A Woman Like Me

Bible Study for Women

A Woman Like Me

Bible Study for Women
To Survive Our Times

Bible Study for Women

A Woman Like Me

Bible Study for Women
To Survive Our Times

By
Minister Onedia N. Gage, Ph. D.

Bible Study for Women

Other Books by Onedia N. Gage, Ph. D.

Are You Ready for 9th Grade . . . Again? A Family's Guide to Success
As We Grow Together Daily Devotional for Expectant Couples
As We Grow Together Prayer Journal for Expectant Couples
As We Grow Together Bible Study: Her Workbook
As We Grow Together Bible Study: His Workbook
The Best 40 Days of My Life: A Journey of Spiritual Renewal
The Blue Print: Poetry for the Soul
From Fat to Fit in 90 Days: A Fitness Journal
From Two to One: The Notebook for the Christian Couple
Hannah's Voice: Powerful Lessons in Prayer
Her Story The Legacy of Her Fight: The Bible Study
Her Story The Legacy of Her Fight: The Devotional
Her Story The Legacy of Her Fight: The Legacy Journal
Her Story The Legacy of Her Fight: Prayers and Journal
I Am.: 90 Days of Powerful Words: Affirmation and Advice for Girls
ILY! A Mother Daughter Relationship Workbook
In Her Own Words: Notebook for the Christian Woman
In 90 Days: What Will You Do?
In Purple Ink: Poetry for the Spirit
In Your Hands: A Dad's Impact on Your Daughter's Self-Esteem
Intensive Couples Retreat: Her Workbook
Intensive Couples Retreat: His Workbook
Living A Whole Life: Sermons Which Prompt, Provoke and Provide Life
Love Letters to God from a Teenage Girl
The Measure of a Woman: The Details of Her Soul
The Notebook: For Me, About Me, By Me
The Notebook for the Christian Teen
On This Journey Daily Devotional for Young People
On This Journey Prayer Journal for Young People
On This Journey Prayer Journal for Young People, Vol. 2
One Day More Than We Deserve Prayer Journal for the Growing Christian
Promises, Promises: A Novel
Queen in the Making: 30 Week Bible Study for Teen Girls
Queen in the Making: 30 Week Bible Study for Teen Girls Leader's Guide
There's a Queen Within: Her Journey to Self—Worth
She Spoke Volumes . . . And Then Some

Six Months of Solitude: The Sanctity of Singleness Notebook
Six Months of Solitude: The Sanctity of Singleness Prayers and Journal
Tools for These Times: Timely Sermons for Uncertain Times
With An Anointed Voice: The Power of Prayer
A Woman Like Me: A Bible Study
A Woman Like Me: A Daily Devotional
A Woman Like Me: A Sermonic Study
Yielded and Submitted: A Woman's Journey for a Life Dedicated to God
Yielded and Submitted: A Woman's Journey for a Life Dedicated to God An Intimate Study
Yielded and Submitted: A Woman's Journey for a Life Dedicated to God Prayers and Journal

The Nehemiah Character Series

Nehemiah and His Basketball
Nehemiah and His Big Sister
Nehemiah and His Bike
Nehemiah and His Flag Football Team
Nehemiah and His Football
Nehemiah and His Golf Clubs
Nehemiah and Math
Nehemiah and the Bully
Nehemiah and the Busy Day
Nehemiah and the Class Field Trip
Nehemiah and the Substitute for the Substitute
Nehemiah Can Swim
Nehemiah Found the Mud
Nehemiah Reads to Mommy
Nehemiah Writes Just Like Mommy
Nehemiah, the Hot Dog, and the Broccoli
Nehemiah's Family Vacation
Nehemiah's Favorite Teacher Returns to School
Nehemiah's First Day of School
Nehemiah's Sister Moved
Nehemiah's Visit to the Hospital

Dedication

Me.

Women like me.

Broken, not quite whole.

Hurt, not quite healed.

Unloved, not quite lovable.

Devastated, not quite diplomatic.

Empty, not quite fillable.

This woman that we need to become should be a priority

And we will become that woman, so that the

Next time we say

A Woman Like Me

We will mean it!

Library of Congress

A Woman Like Me:

Bible Study for Women

All Rights Reserved © 2020
Onedia N. Gage, Ph. D.

No part of this of book may be reproduced or transmitted in
Any form or by any means, graphic, electronic, or mechanical,
Including photocopying, recording, taping, or by any
Information storage or retrieval system, without the
Permission in writing from the publisher.

Purple Ink, Inc. Press
For Information address:
Purple Ink, Inc
P O Box 300113
Houston, TX 77230
www.purpleink.net ♦ www.onediagage.com
onediagage@purpleink.net ♦ onediagage@onediagage.com

ISBN:

978-0-9801002-6-6

Printed in United States

What God Has to Say

Hannah
1 Samuel 1:12-16 New International Version (NIV)

[12] As she kept on praying to the Lord, Eli observed her mouth. [13] Hannah was praying in her heart, and her lips were moving but her voice was not heard. Eli thought she was drunk [14] and said to her, "How long are you going to stay drunk? Put away your wine."

[15] "Not so, my lord," Hannah replied, "I am a woman who is deeply troubled. I have not been drinking wine or beer; I was pouring out my soul to the Lord. [16] Do not take your servant for a wicked woman; I have been praying here out of my great anguish and grief."

Elizabeth
Luke 1:24-25 New International Version (NIV)

[24] After this his wife Elizabeth became pregnant and for five months remained in seclusion. [25] "The Lord has done this for me," she said. "In these days he has shown his favor and taken away my disgrace among the people."

Ruth
Ruth 1:16-18 New International Version (NIV)

[16] But Ruth replied, "Don't urge me to leave you or to turn back from you. Where you go I will go, and where you stay I will stay. Your people will be my people and your God my God. [17] Where you die I will die, and there I will be buried. May the Lord deal with me, be it ever so severely, if even death separates you and me." [18] When Naomi realized that Ruth was determined to go with her, she stopped urging her.

Eve
Genesis 3:1 New International Version (NIV)
The Fall

3 Now the serpent was more crafty than any of the wild animals the LORD God had made. He said to the woman, "Did God really say, 'You must not eat from any tree in the garden'?"

[16] To the woman He said,

"I will make your pains in childbearing very severe; with painful labor you will give birth to children. Your desire will be for your husband, and he will rule over you."

[20] Adam named his wife Eve, because she would become the mother of all the living.

Mary
Luke 10:38—42

Esther
Esther 2:12—18

Naomi
Ruth 1:21—22

Bathsheba
2 Samuel 11:2—5; 12:19, 24—25

Job's Wife
Job 2:9—10; 42:10—17

Gomer
Hosea 1:2—3; 2

The Samaritan Woman/The Woman at the Well
John 4:1—26

Woman with 12 Year Issue of Blood
Luke 8:40—50

Sarai
Genesis 16:1—4; 21:1—2

Noah's Wife
Genesis 6:9, 18—19; 7:1—5; 8:11

Hagar
Genesis 16:7—16; 21:17

Bible Study for Women

A Woman Like Me

Dear God,

I pray You bless me. I know that my silence in this season has its issues, however I am devastated about how my life is progressing. The need for this study comes at a time when I need affirmation and other women like me need the same. WE need to hear from You. WE need to see Your hand of protection over our lives and that of our families. WE need a miracle in our careers and finances. We have dreams and goals that we need to see to develop and materialize.

WE need to be able to see the realization of our prayers. WE need to have what we pray for and be the women You have called for and make sure that we are able to testify to that fact that You are the God that we pray to and attest to and worship to and witness about. WE need something new to witness about.

I pray that You bless the women will read, share and be blessed and spiritually fed from this study. I labored and was uplifted. I toiled and was replenished. I whined and You offered me some grace. I wept and You sent me a shoulder. I studied and You gave me a retreat.

Lord, I am questioning the lessons and the outcome. I am considering the world and our current situation. We are under the attack of disease. What message are You sending? What do You want from us? What do You want us to do now?

Lord, thank You for entrusting me with this book, these words, and this study. I pray that I listen to Your voice to share the correct words that You want seen. Lord, thank You for using me! Lord, I so want to impress You by obeying You!

I pray for these blessings in Jesus' name.
Amen.

Bible Study for Women

Dear Woman Like Me:

I know that you are like me in many ways and that is SCARY. I am certainly on edge, in a bad head space, need to hear from the God who declared His love for me, but I cannot see it because I need it to look like something else. As a woman, we have many roles and jobs, desires and dreams, however we will only achieve those to which He consents. I am certain that He heard me but He tells me no or wait. At some point, He tells me yes and then we may be in real trouble. So if you are really like me, we are dangerous and in trouble.

With that in mind, we need to heal. My prayer is that your healing is instrumental and inspirational to others whose paths you will cross. In the meantime, as you work through these questions, I hope that you also allow these words to minister to you so that you are whole emotionally and spiritually—better than ever before.

Use these pages to address your authentic self in an outlandish manner. You are a bold, courageous, trustworthy, and special woman. You have a message but it is restricted underneath all of that hurt, pain, brokenness, devastation, and emptiness. Let this time be spent seeking God for all that He is and all that He wants for you.

One of my favorite Bible verses is 1 Corinthians 13:13, the Message version, which reads: "Love extravagantly." This is a great time for you to remove the boundaries of your love and love outrageously with an understanding that you can NEVER run out. You are not the supplier of your own love. God is. Love because He loves you.

Further, love heals. In this love and healing, you can overcome. Use this time to heal from everything. Surrender it all to God like you have never done before.

Bible Study for Women

I pray for your wholeness. Wellness. Spirit. Love. Mission. Vision. Dreams. And achievements. This is part of your legacy. What you do next is more important than what happened. What happened should cause something BIG to happen next. Don't block the BIG! It is the best part of you!

Use this Bible Study to address your feelings, fears, and what you think about yourself and God. The questions are provocative, pensive, piercing, productive, and powerful. Do not cut yourself short. Leave it all on the paper. Use your words. Give yourself permission to grow through this experience. Look at your life and consider the options. Decide to live and escape that which holds you hostage, including yourself.

Leave a HUGE legacy! Start with yourself!!

I look forward to hearing from you. Feel free to share with me as you journey. You can follow me on twitter @onediangage, email onediagage@onediagage.com, facebook.com/onediagageministries, blogtalkradio.com/onediagage, and youtube.com/onediagage. www.onediagage.com

I can hardly wait!

In His Service!

Onedia N Gage

Minister Onedia N. Gage, Ph. D.

Study Covenant

I vow to . . .

Give my whole self to the study.

Fully immerse myself into this so that I can grow, spiritually, emotionally, and mentally.

Address my true issues about my life and its faults and its directions.

Address my true victories about my life and its greatness and how to continue.

Be transparent about my needs and fears.

Offer myself as a living sacrifice, open to hearing from God in a mighty way.

Signed   Date

_____   _____

Instructions for Use

Share your whole self.

Prayerfully.

Listen to heart as you read and respond.

Share what will help others.

Give this all of you.

Be transparent to yourself so you can see what God is doing within you, for you, and around you.

Bible Study for Women

Table of Contents

Prayer 15

Letters 17

Covenant 19

Instructions 21

Poem: "The Measure of a Woman" 25

The Bible Study 27

    Week One: Love 29

    Week Two: Peace 59

    Week Three: Faith 83

    Week Four: Trust 107

    Week Five: Prayer 127

    Week Six: Wisdom 153

Appendix — 203

- Your Testimony — 204
- The Names of God — 206
- Prayer Directions — 209
- Prayer Request List/Journal — 209

Resources — 213

- —other books

Acknowledgements — 215

About the Woman — 217

THE MEASURE OF A WOMAN
By Onedia N. Gage

The Measure of a Woman

    What is the width of her spirit

    What is the depth of her mind

    What is the weight of her heart

    What is the volume of her body

    What is the capacity of her mind

    What is the speed of her thoughts

    What is the circumference of her hugs

    What is the breadth of her love

    How many inches does she let you within the boundaries of her heart

    How many feet until she reaches forgiveness

    What is the slope of her attitude

    What is the velocity of her meekness

The Measure of a Woman

    She thinks critically

    She plans carefully

    She speaks dynamically

    She loves passionately

    She lives authentically

> She moves fearlessly
>
> She leads humbly
>
> She fears God

Experience the Measure of a Woman

> Her love
>
> Her fears
>
> Her tears
>
> Her victories
>
> Her power
>
> Her influence
>
> Her motivation

Invest in the Measure of a Woman

> Create for her a loving environment
>
> Create for her a safe place

Go the distance for the Measure of a Woman

The Measure of a Woman

> Defines love
>
> Defies opposition

Declares independence

Decorates hearts

Demands chemistry

The Measure of a Woman

Reprinted from <u>The Measure of a Woman: The Details of Her Soul</u>

The Bible Study

Week One: Love

Memory Verse:

39 She had a sister called Mary, who sat at the Lord's feet listening to what he said.

Luke 10:39

Love is a small word but it a large emotion and a huge scope of work. Real love is based on action—it is a verb. Love takes action.

John 3:16 defines the extravagant love that Paul commands us in 1 Corinthians 13:13 MSG.
Love is a command which Jesus is the demonstration of the definition. I could say that four more times, four different ways, because it is true. Love is not a scarce commodity nor an endangered species. Love is essential for everyone. Love is not discriminatory by age.

How can you live effectively without God's love?

How can you live effectively without loving others?

How can you share God with others without love—the demonstration and the words?

During our study this week, we will study love.

Day 1: God's love

       John 3:16

Day 2: Jesus' love

       Romans 5:8

Day 3: Your love

       1 Corinthians

Day 4: Love to others

       Romans 12:9

Day 5: Love of others

       1 Peter 4:8

Day One: God's Love

John 3:16

³ For God so loved the world that He gave His only Son, that whosoever believes in Him should not perish but have everlasting life.

It's easy to hear and understand God's love. You can easily identify and define God's love. But do you believe in God's love? What does God's love feel like, look like, and mean?

When God loves us, it seems unreal, unrealistic, and impossible. The first reason is that we don't believe that we should be loved. We define love differently that God. God loves us because we don't deserve love. We love when people have earned our love, by whatever definition we are using which is far from consistent.

Dictionary.com defines love as the benevolent affection of God for His creatures, or the reverent affection due from them to God. God defines love as John 3:16, Romans 5:5, Exodus 34:6—7, Deuteronomy 7:9, and Deuteronomy 7:6—8. God entered into a covenant of love with us through the Israelites He delivered out of Egypt.

Then He affirmed that love through Noah and the Ark. He then reenacted that love when He kept the promise of a Savior in the birth, death and resurrection of Jesus Christ.

God's love is not something we can actually create because we are not selfless enough or visionary enough to do so. However, what we do have is His love, we can give away freely because we will never run out. He also authorizes His love through your ability to love yourself.

Bible Study for Women

When we consider God's love, we need to look at the origin of that love. Love defend by God is a love that is everlasting and a love which cannot be measured.

Deuteronomy 6:5 reads: "Love the Lord Your God with all of Your heart and soul and mind." God can command that of You because that is how He loves you.

1. Explain how you know that God loves you.

_____
_____
_____
_____
_____

2. How do you explain His love to others?

_____
_____
_____
_____
_____

3. What do you say to others and do for yourself when you may doubt His love or His presence?

_____
_____
_____
_____
_____

God is the ultimate demonstration of love. 1. He led the Israelites; 2. He re-created the world; 3. He saved Joseph and consequently his entire family; 4. He sent us Jesus; 5. He sent the Holy Spirit; 6. He created you; 7. He left us with an instruction manual: The Bible.

4. What did He do to demonstrate His love for you specifically?

_____
_____
_____
_____
_____

John 3:16 reads: For God so loved the world that He gave His Only Son that whosoever believes in Him would not perish but would have everlasting life. God promised us a Savior in the Old Testament. God knew that we would need Jesus. He sent His Son in a perfect way to do a big job, to save an ungrateful world, so that we may live.

5. Could you think of any bigger gift than that? Can God give you anything bigger or better?

6. When you consider Mary and Joseph's job, could you do it? If so, how and why? If not, why?

God commands us to love our neighbors as ourselves. The command is non—negotiable, however, we act like it is. One of the reasons that we cannot love others is because we barely love ourselves. God gives us permission to love ourselves because He first loved us.

7. Would God approve of how you feel about yourself? If not, how can you upgrade that feeling/opinion?

_____
_____
_____
_____
_____

8. Who do you not love that you should but do not? How can you improve that disposition?

_____
_____
_____
_____
_____

9. Are you afraid to love? Are you afraid to love others?

_____
_____
_____
_____
_____

Job had an outrageous task! He endured the test of satan at the permission of God. It seems that this would never end, however, after a while, Job was doubly restored with the blessings in his life. What Job does for all of us is to offer us an understanding of what God expects from us when we are presented with various adversities. Job did exactly what we would do: ask God questions based on our limited vision and knowledge of why we are suffering if He loves us. God answered Job for three chapters. These answers were in part questions for Job and this was surprised Job because he was not expecting any response from God.

10. What had God done which demonstrated His love for you which surprised you the most?

___

11. Based on Job's behavior, what will you do differently?

___

12. Which questions answers surprised you most between God and Job?

_____
_____
_____
_____
_____

13. Did God love Job? What evidence supports you answer?

_____
_____
_____
_____
_____

God demonstrates His love for us.

God has poured out His love into our hearts (Romans 5:5).

14. Because God poured out His love into our hearts, what do you think that God expects you to do with that unlimited reservoir of love?

_____
_____

Bible Study for Women

_____
_____
_____

15. Who do you think that he expects you to share that love with?

_____
_____
_____
_____
_____

16. What does it take to share that love with yourself and others? Why has it been difficult to love yourself and others? When can you start loving?

_____
_____
_____
_____
_____

17. Share a time when God's love has lifted you from a low place?

_____

A Woman Like Me

Write a love letter to God.

Day Two: Jesus' Love

Romans 5:8

[8] But God demonstrates his own love for us in this: While we were still sinners, Christ died for us.

Ephesians 3:14—21

John 14:15, 21, 23, 24a

Jesus teaches a special type of love—one that no one else can replicate! He died for us to live and be forgiven for our transgression. The Lord said that because of His great love for us, He gave us His Son to die for us. That is a unique love. Can you think of a reason that you would offer your child up as a sacrifice? Do you know anyone who would sacrifice their child to save people—the whole world—willingly? I don't.

Jesus' love was sacrificial—it was given with a cost. Jesus demonstrates love. Jesus teaches love. Jesus is love!

1. Do you know that Jesus loves you? How do you know? (Are there times when you doubt that He loves you?)

_____
_____
_____
_____
_____

2. Can anyone else love you like Jesus does? Why?

3. Do you share Jesus' love with other people? Why or why not? Who can you share it with?

Romans 5:8 declares God's love for us that while were still sinners, Jesus still died for us. God and Jesus did this knowing that we would still sin even after His death, even after His burial, and even still after resurrection.

4. Rewrite this in your own words. What does this verse mean to you? Who will you share the verse with and why?

_____

_____

_____

_____

Some of my favorite verses of the Bible can be found in Ephesians 3:14—21.
Paul opens these verses in prayer. He prays this beautiful, powerful, and heartfelt prayer and shares some great lessons about the love of Jesus. Because of the power of the Holy Spirit because of the will of God, Jesus can occupy our hearts with our faith. The next point which should be made is that we are all from the same God, Jesus and Holy Spirit. Keeping in mind that God created each of us, so when He says 'derives its name,' I blush.

You have power which you do not use or access, and you are not even sure why. What about the power that He gives us that He just waits for us to access?

5. What does that power do? What do you need to use that power for? Why don't we access that power more often?

_____

_____

_____

_____

_____

Bible Study for Women

When you consider the measure of God's love: wide, long, high, and deep—that's the measure of infinity. Volume is measured by length, width and height. Area is measured by length and width. When you consider the measure represented by height, length, width, and depth, then you cannot doubt the love of God.

6. What has to happen so that you can recognize the love of God?

___

God's love surpasses our knowledge and understanding.

7. When has God loved you but you were confused about why God loved you in spite of what you do or do not do?

___

8. When does God love you but you don't love yourself?

_____
_____
_____
_____
_____

John 14:15, 20, 23, 24a

God defines love differently. God describes it in the context of obedience. John 14:15 reads, "If you love Me, then you will obey My command." In Geometry, this is called a conditional statement. The conclusion, the phrase that follows the 'then,' is what should happen after the hypothesis, the phrase after the word 'if.' Also, that statement should be true. There are some other parts to the logical conditional statement. One such statement is the converse, which is the opposite of the condition. The converse of that statement is 'If you are obedient to My command, then you love Me.' Is that statement true? The inverse of the statement is 'If you do not love Me, then you will not obey My commands.' The last statement is the contrapositive is 'If you do not obey My command, the you do not love Me.' The statements are true based on the logic of the statement, however in the way and real world, the conditional and converse statements are actually false. While the inverse and contrapositive are true. The fact is that we are not obedient. Because we are not obedient, then we cannot claim that we love Him.

9. How can we correct our behavior to demonstrate our love for Jesus?

10. What has to happen before you can choose love over self and disobedience?

Admittedly, we are not Jesus, so vastly different. However, there are ways which we are like Jesus.

11. List some ways which you have demonstrated the attributes of Jesus.

12. Read John 14:15, 20, 23, and 24a. Use these scriptures to reflect on how you are disobedient and decide how you will stop being disobedient.

_____
_____
_____
_____
_____

Jesus, help me love You enough so that I willingly obey!

Day Three: Your Love
1 Corinthians 13
[13]Love extravagantly. (MSG)

Paul gives these verses as a prescription of love. This is no easy feat—not at all. Paul gives us some excellent lessons on love.

Verses 1—3, the word states that if I don't have love, then I have nothing. That may seem harsh, however if you do not love, then what is your contribution? What is your reason for not loving?

Not loving is a decision—one made intentionally, usually because of an issue or incident. Love is natural. Love is a demonstration. Love is on exhibit, naturally. Love is not forced.

1. When do you have problem with loving (yourself and others)? Why?

    _____
    _____
    _____
    _____

2. If you have stopped loving, then what is your contribution?

    _____
    _____
    _____

3. When you made that decision to not love, did you consider what that cost those that love you?

Verses 4—7 offers the definition of love with direct examples. When you consider the definition of patient, are you? Are you kind? Are you envious? Do you boast? Are you too proud? Do you dishonor others? Are you self—seeking? Are you easily angered? Do you keep back of the wrong doings of others? Do you rejoice with the truth? Do you protect, trust, hope, and persevere? All the time? When you consider these definitions, there may be some of these characteristics are difficult for you. How do you know? How will you improve in those areas?

4. What is God calling us to do and to improve upon?

5. What does it take to love according to those scriptures?

6. What have we been commanded to love but we are not able to love? Why not?

Verses 8—12 teaches us that love never fails. We don't know that failure because God's love and Jesus' redemption through love saves us because of love. Nothing but love matters. So much so that love will overshadow all other things. God has the option to overlook all the 'good' that we did and will do because we did not do it with love.

7. Do you really understand God's command of love on your life? What does it take to understand His love, internalize it and then share it?

_____

_____

_____

_____

_____

Verse 13 is The Message Bible, reads, "But for right now, until that completeness, we have three things to do to lead as toward that consummation: Trust steadily in God, hope unswervingly, love extravagantly. And the best of the three is love.

I want you to investigate the 'love extravagantly' phrase. LOVE extravagantly! Read that several times. As you consider that love is a verb, a part of speech indicating that action is required, love means that you do some things to demonstrate love and to share love and to be love.

Then the word love is coupled with extravagantly, an adverb, is defined as spending much more time than is necessary or wise; wasteful; exceeding the bounds of reason, as actions, demands, opinions, or passions. This phrase can be translated to love exceeding the bounds of reason; a wasteful love; loving more than is necessary or wise.

I define loving others extravagantly as above their means and yours. Keep loving when it is scary, or ridiculous, undeserved or unwise. Love when love is inconvenient, unnecessary, and seems that love will never be returned.

8. Love extravagantly. God did. Jesus did. Can you? Will you? What does it take for you to love? To love extravagantly?

_____

_____

_____

_____

9. Who do you need help loving? You are created to love and are assigned to love others.

_____

_____

_____

_____

_____

1 Corinthians 13.

Please replace your name in the blank. Read the modified verses with your name out loud.

13 If I speak in the tongues of men or of angels, but do not have love, I am only a resounding gong or a clanging cymbal. ² If I have the gift of prophecy and can fathom all mysteries and all knowledge, and if I have a faith that can move mountains, but do not have love, I am nothing. ³ If I give all I possess to the poor and give over my body to hardship that I may boast, but do not have love, I gain nothing.

⁴ _____ is patient, _____ is kind. _____ does not envy, _____ does not boast, _____ is not proud. ⁵ _____ does not dishonor others, _____ is not self-seeking, _____ is not easily angered, _____ keeps no record of wrongs. ⁶ _____ does not delight in evil but rejoices with the truth. ⁷ _____ always protects, always trusts, always hopes, always perseveres.

⁸ Love never fails. But where there are prophecies, they will cease; where there are tongues, they will be stilled; where there is knowledge, it will pass away. ⁹ For we know in part and we prophesy in part, ¹⁰ but when completeness comes, what is in part disappears. ¹¹ When I was a child, I talked like a child, I thought like a child, I reasoned like a child. When I became a man, I put the ways of childhood behind me. ¹² For now we see only a reflection as in a mirror; then we shall see face to face. Now I know in part; then I shall know fully, even as I am fully known.

¹³ And now these three remain: faith, hope and love. But the greatest of these is love.

Day Four: The Love to Others

Romans 12:9

⁹ Love must be sincere. Hate what is evil; cling to what is good.

John 13:34—35

"Love is a battlefield." Lyrics made popular from a song in the 80's. "Love thy neighbor as yourself." Popular scripture from over 2000 years ago. Not the same concept. Similarly, the world teaches and promotes, hate, indifference, and anti-love. Jesus commands love your neighbor as yourself, love one another, and no greater love than when you will lay your life down for a friend.

Romans 12:9 reads: "Love must be sincere. Hate what is evil; cling to what is good."

First important point of loving others is to be sincere. That is difficult when you do not understand how love benefits you even when you don't receive love in return.

Sincere is not what is in it for me, but what does the other person need. Putting another person's needs before yours is sincerity.

1. How can you be more sincere as you love others?

_____
_____
_____
_____

Second is selfless. Again, putting someone else before yourself—their needs, their desires, their love, and their well—being. The calling we have is to be like Christ. That calling includes loving like Him. That is the hardest thing that we will ever do. His demonstration of sacrificial love is so that we can do the same.

2. What conditions is your love based upon? What does your love cost others? What does a person have to do so that you will love them?

_____
_____
_____
_____
_____

3. Do you love at 100%? If not, what is your actual percentage? Is that based on who the person is—someone who know versus stranger versus stranger that you need something from?

_____
_____
_____
_____
_____

John 15:13 reads "Greater love has no one than this: to lay down one's life for one's friends." Who does God intend for us to love at this level? There is our answer, then there's God's answer. Our answer is just a few people, but those people can fall off of that list if one issue happens. God's answer is just the opposite: EVERYBODY!

When you recall that Jesus died for the sinners who killed and betrayed Him, it is God's will to do this for everyone, no exceptions.

4. Why does God want us to love all people? What does it take for you to love at the level God requires?

_____

_____

_____

_____

_____

Jesus issues a command to love in John 13:34—35.

34 "A new command I give you: Love one another. As I have loved you, so you must love one another. 35 By this everyone will know that you are my disciples, if you love one another."

5. What do we do to our relationship with God when we ignore Jesus' command to love? How can we repair that relationship?

_____

_____

_____
_____
_____

Jesus, help me to love others the way that You do and as You have commanded. Amen.

Day Five: The Love of Others

1 Peter 4:8

"Above all, love each other deeply, because love covers over a multitude of sins."

Love, authentic love, does so much to people and for people. Loving others deeply requires selflessness. Likewise, love covers the sins of others and creates a space for than to survive their sins. Forgiveness is the result of love.

1. What does it take for you to love deeply?

_____
_____
_____
_____
_____

One of the most important things to do is to accept love from others, especially strangers.

Keep in mind that God said that He would send people to assist you, bear your burdens, and offer you His peace. In order to do that, God uses people. The people that He sends will not always know why they are there, they just know that they have the means and heart to help you and meet your needs. Accept your help. Graciously. Stop questioning. Yes, they will come from out of nowhere. This is your warning.

The love of others is also designed to restore your faith. The love of others keeps you from walking away from God. The love of others changes your attitude. The love of others could save your life. The love of others allows you to accept yourself. As is. Without modifications. The love of others inspires you to keep taking the daily steps required to move ahead.

The love of others reminds you that God has not forgotten you and that you are important to Him. The love of others brings out the best in you. The love of others lifts your head, enriches your heart, and stimulates your spirit.

The love of others is God's message that He is still in control.

The love of others will scare you, but not scar you—rather heals and shapes your mind toward God at the next level.

2. Recall a time when God's love showed up in some unexpected people.

_____
_____
_____
_____
_____

3. How will you position yourself better to receive the love of others the way God asked you to?

4. What are you praying for that may cause God to send unexpected people?

Be prepared to accept the love of others. Start now.

God, help me to see the love of others as love and as love sent by you. Amen.

Week Two: Peace

Memory Verse:

30 The righteous will never be uprooted,
but the wicked will not remain in the land.

Proverbs 10:30

Peace is defined differently by most people. Peace is also experienced differently by most people. Peace is demonstrated differently by most people. Peace is sought differently by all people. Peace is differently important to all people. Pease is practiced differently and inconsistently by all people. The peace we need, we often reject. The peace we desire is the very peace we treat counterproductively. When we should be peaceful, we decide against it. When we are served peace, we send it back. But why?

We need peace! We need peace to survive. We need peace to hear from God. We need to peace to love—ourselves and others. We need peace to experience God and Jesus. We need peace to understand God's and Jesus' demonstration of peace.

It is nearly impossible to understand peace without a foundation of peace. How do you achieve peace? How do you acquire peace? How do you share peace? How do you experience peace when you are experiencing a storm? How do you accept peace when you just spoke against peace?

What does peace do to propel your spirit forward? How does peace assist you with being peaceful, while rejecting turmoil?

Why does God provide His peace when we are subject to reject His peace?

Peace defined. Peace demonstrated. Peace practiced. Peace challenged. Peace experience. Peace stimulates life. Peace stimulates healing. Peace produces trust. Peace entreats love. Peace heals. Peace promotes unity.

Jesus teaches peace. Jesus commands peace. Jesus promotes peace. Jesus provides peace. What do you need to be peaceful?

Day 1: Peace Defined

    Psalm 29:11

Day 2: Peace Demonstrated

    John 16:33

Day 3: Peace Practiced

    James 3:18

Day 4: Peace Challenged
    Matthew 10:13

Day 5: Peace Achieved/Accomplished
    Proverbs 10:30

Day One: Peace Defined

Psalm 29:11

[11] The LORD gives strength to his people;
    the LORD blesses his people with peace.

Peace is defined as a state of mutual harmony between people of groups, especially in personal relations. Peace is also seen as a war—free agreement between nations, tribes, and neighborhoods, especially those which were previously at war.

Peace is also the ability to be internally at rest. Peace is the opposite of cantankerous behavior and an unrestful spirit, which could be a spirit which seeks and attracts turmoil and other disturbances. Peace does not exist in persons who are continuously the leader of trouble, drama, and strife.
So now that we know what peace is not, let us examine what it is.

God and Jesus provides peace! Peace is not something that we can give ourselves, but peace requires our participation.

1. Define peace. In your own words and interpretation.

_____
_____
_____
_____

2. Provide examples of peace.

___

3. Provide non—examples of peace.

___

4. What can you do to avoid yourself—inflicted lack of peace?

___

Peace is a gift from God. Jesus demonstrates what peace looks like and feels like. Jesus offers peace that is indescribable.

Jesus is introduced to the world as the Prince of Peace (Isaiah 9:6). This defines Him as the ambassador and the giver of peace. This peace is hard to explain but when you have this peace, you know it. Jesus' peace is best experienced. Jesus' peace keeps you from going crazy. His place keeps you from staying awake when worry has taken over your spirit. His peace keeps you from quitting. His peace keeps you close to Him when you actually want to run. His peace begs you when you are alone and lonely, scared and scarred. His peace controls your mind, your heart, and your spirit. His place promotes love: for Him, self, and others.

As we define peace, consider God's invention for the peace experience. Peace is not fleeting, but instead a comfort that only He can provide, which He provides to further facilitate His will.

God blesses you with His peace. Psalm 29:11

Peace can only dwell where righteousness exists. Psalm 85:10.

Peace is an element of a Fruit of the Spirit. Galatians 5:22.

He will keep you in perfect peace for those with a steadfast mind a trusting disposition. Isaiah 26:3.

He is peace and He give it to you at all times and in every way. 2 Thessalonians 3:16.

Peace is an inheritance from Jesus. This peace keeps you from having a troubled heart and is designed to cast out fear. John 14:27.

God created.

Jesus gifted.

5. Describe how peace makes you feel based on how you realized it is given and what peace is and does.

___

6. How will you share the definition of peace?

___

7. Where does His peace lead you? Ephesians 6:15.

___

Day 2: Peace Demonstrated

John 16:33

³³ "I have told you these things, so that in me you may have peace. In this world you will have trouble. But take heart! I have overcome the world."

James 3:18

Colossians 3:15

Romans 3:17

Psalm 34:14

Psalm 119:165

1 Samuel 1:17

Isaiah 57:19

Psalm 37:11

Peace, similar to love, is a verb. God demonstrates His investment for us through His provision of peace. Demonstrating peace is quite a task. Peace requires you to seek it. (Psalm 34:14) Peace can only be demonstrated if you seek it and desire it. Peace requires meekness (Psalm 37:11). Haughtiness does not produce or harbor peace. Peace can be requested on your behalf by others. (1 Samuel 1:17).

God is speaking about and to Israel regarding their behavior and attitude about what He desires for them to do, but they were disobedient. Once He finished this monologue, where God restores them, admits His anger and disgust for them and their actions, God promised that He will heal them. Finally, God promised to grant them peace. (Isaiah 57:19). God provides peace. Jesus demonstrates peace and peaceful behavior and a peaceful spirit. Peace creates comfort.

1. What does God do to demonstrate peace?

___

2. What does Jesus do to demonstrate peace?

___

3. What does God expect you to do to demonstrate peace?

___

4. Are you doing all of that in order to be peaceful?

___

5. Who do you know who is peaceful? Why do you feel that way? What have they done to let you see their peacefulness?

___

Demonstrating peace is a journey rather than a destination. Peace is like breathing—it has to continue so that you can live. Peace is also gift giving and relieves you from strife and dis—ease. Peace rescues you from the depths of depression which would like to possess you. Peace keeps you from hurting, hurting yourself, and hurting others. Peace reminds you of your beauty and your worth, your value, and your self—esteem.

Peace requires maturity and God reminds you that He is in full control. Peace surprises you. (Colossians 3:15) Peace rules and resides in your heart. Its source is the place where you harbor the best and most emotions.

Peace is contagious. You can recall instances where the situation was about to get out of hand and the Peacemaker shows up and all of the drama fades. Nobody really understood, not even the person who is used as the Peacemaker's representative.

Peace is what we should seek. Peace is synonymous with meekness. Peace is not easy.

6. What could you do to be more peaceful?

_____
_____
_____
_____
_____

Day Three: Peace Practiced

James 3:18

[18] Peacemakers who sow in peace reap a harvest of righteousness.

There are choices in this life: one is peace and one is the opposite of peace.

How do you practice peace? In elementary school, you may have been taught that you should not define a word with the word itself. So the answer of being peaceful is in order to practice peace is unreasonable and not necessarily helpful.

Practice peace by silence, avoiding cantankerous behavior or verbiage, and listening to the whole situation before responding or reaching a judgement. Peace when practiced is a demonstration of compassion and forgiveness. No, practicing peace is not easy, however required.

Peace practiced is best defined as deciding to walk away from an argument, or choosing to be the mediator between quarreling friends rather than siding with one over the other, seeking to bring the two back together.

Peace practiced is being optimistic about something which has been previously known as terrible. Peace practiced listens to others so that you can understand what others need and what others are going through. Peace practiced translates to you being a source of peace and wisdom, prayers and wholesome words.

1. Who among you is peaceful? Why do you perceive that they are peaceful?

_____
_____
_____
_____

Jesus practices peace when He identifies His betrayer. Humans do not normally do that. We would have confronted our Judas', fought our Judas', slander our Judas', and more.

2. How did you feel about what Jesus did for Judas?

_____
_____
_____
_____
_____

Jesus demonstrates peace when He forgave Judas and the people who hung Him on that cross.

3. Can you forgive someone who has willfully hurt and betrayed you?

_____
_____

4. Who do you need to forgive and whom do you need to be forgiven by so that you are able to practice peace?

5. What will you have to change in order to practice peace?

1 Peter 5:7 reads, "Cast your cares on Him because He cares for you." Practicing peace means not having anxiety or dwelling in stress. These areas are certainly not peaceful. Peace cannot exist where anxiety also resides. This is not of God and Jesus.

Is this difficult? Yes. Is it possible? Absolutely. How do you avoid anxiety? Evaluate why you are anxious. Decide on why this is causing anxiety. Then decide to eliminate the anxiety. Then eliminate it. Easier said than done because there is a decision and commitment involved, however the real decision is for peace. Is your peace worth releasing your anxiety? Certainly!

The company you keep will impact your peace. Are your friends peaceful? Or are they always in an uproar? Is your family peaceful? Or are they always experiencing drama?

Peace does not mean that nothing ever happens. Peace practiced means that when conflict and drama arises, you remain calm, use logic, and operate in love to reach a solution.

Peace practiced is finding a solution which is equitable, and decent.

6. What can you do to practice peace at home?

_____
_____
_____
_____
_____

7. What can you do to practice peace at work?

_____

8. What can you do to practice peace at home within your larger family?

9. What can you do to practice peace with your friends?

Day Four: Peace Challenged

Matthew 10:13

[13] If the home is deserving, let your peace rest on it; if it is not, let your peace return to you.

Jeremiah 6:14
Job 3:26
Judges 3:30
Isaiah 57:21
Psalm 120:6—7

In this life, your peace will be challenged. Between the daily challenges and the political unrest and your personal challenges, there will be days when you will question the very definition of peace.

Job is suffering with afflictions and is feeling quite distant from God. The Job 3:26 verse speaks to his disdain, discontent, and discomfort.

Have you felt like that—like nothing can be done to enjoy some peace? I believe we all do.

1. What has been a time when your life has been the most unpeaceful?

_____
_____
_____
_____
_____

2. What was your scripture and prayer during this season?

_____
_____
_____
_____

3. How was life when peace was present and available and undisturbed? Were you thankful? Did you recognize that peace?

_____
_____
_____
_____

Be thankful for that peace. Be thankful when your peace is challenged as well. When your peace is challenged, consider your behavior. Isaiah 57:21 reads, "There is no peace for the wicked, says my God."

4. In what areas is your peace most challenged? Why?

_____

5. How can you reduce that challenge?

6. How do you recover from a challenged peace?

Job's story had relevance here. His peace was challenged and he asked God several questions. He also seeks to prove his point that he didn't do anything to deserve this 'punishment' and lack of peace. His

friends respond to him, but when God speaks out of the storm (Job 38—41) and lets Job know that He reigns supreme. God addresses the issues that Job raised and He chastised Job's friends as well.
In all of this discourse, we are to understand that God can and will interrupt your peace whenever He decides, for whatever reason He decides.

Job learned many lessons in these rough 42 chapters.

7. What are you to learn when your peace is at risk or completely disturbed?

_____

_____

_____

_____

_____

You also impact the peace of others. Matthew 10:13 reads, "that if a house deserves your peace then offer it." How do we determine if someone deserves our peace? Everyone does deserve, until they don't. Give away peace. It does not cost you anything to give it away because it was freely given to you and it's not replenished by you either.

God's definition of peace is wellness in your soul. The challenge to your soul is the only way to challenge your actual peace.

Job did not know why he was suffering because he had not done so . . . ever! This was just to baffle his mind, to cause a little conflict, to test his biblical knowledge, and to offer a true test of who he really was . . . his character. God was protecting his soul, where his inner peace exists. A disturbance of your inner peace causes actual destruction, not the threat thereof.

So ask yourself the next time your peace is 'challenged,' is this real or a façade? Is my soul up for negotiation? If not, then move on accordingly.

8. With that in mind, when has your peace actually been disturbed or challenged?

_____
_____
_____
_____
_____

Job was restored. And affirmed.

Amen.

Day Five: Peace Achieved/Accomplished

Proverbs 14:30

[30] A heart at peace gives life to the body,
   but envy rots the bones.

Jude 1:2
Luke 2:29; 12:51
Numbers 6:26
Romans 12:18, 14:19
Psalm 37
Job 22:21
Job 42
Philippians 4:7

Our superficial definition of peace is based on our daily lives being as we desire: with wealth, material evidence of a well—taken care of life, health, and any other accoutrement we desire. But that maybe the definition of blessed, rather than peace.

The reason we don't know if we have peace or how to be peaceful is that we really don't know what it is. So we cannot actually experience it or recognize it.

Peace had many definitions based on the usage as a noun, verb, and adjective. They are different, yet aligned. The common thread is God and how you relate to Him.

You decide to be peace and to experience peace and are able to recognize peace by being peaceful, rather than wicked, evil, and living out of God's will.

There's a distinct difference between being a repenting sinner and a wicked being. One of them will experience peace and the other will not.

Peace is accessible so it can be achieved and accomplished.

Here is a self—test:
- Are you wicked?
- Do you seek to bring harm to others even when they deserve it?
- Do you need sleeping pills to sleep?
- Are you always checking for your enemy?
- Are you always seeking position over others?
- Did you gain power through deceptive means?

If you had to think about these questions, then you are not peace, peaceful, or peace—seeking.

The other side: Are you:
- Optimistic?
- Peace—seeking?
- Forgiving?
- Waiting on God?
- Merciful?
- Trusting?
- Loving?

- Do you sleep well at night?
- Do you apologize when you have done another person wrong?
- Do you recognize when you have harmed another?
- Do you seek to be a better person everyday?

That is when peace is accomplished and achieved.

1. What can you do to make sure that you are peaceful, peace, and a peace—seeker?

_____
_____
_____
_____

Amen.

Week Three: Faith

Memory Verse:

31 Immediately Jesus reached out his hand and caught him. "You of little faith," he said, "why did you doubt?"
32 And when they climbed into the boat, the wind died down.

Matthew 14:31—32

Faith is almost as ambiguous as peace. Faith is a belief without ANY evidence. This is done through deed, thoughts, and demonstration. When we consider the definition of faith through the life of some special Biblical characters, we have to consider David, Mary, Paul, Peter, and Esther.

Faith is required to please God, to get His attention, to keep His attention, and to prove your sincerity to Him.

Faith is invisible while evident. Faith is hard to have, but much harder to defend when you choose not to have faith.

So how do you learn faith? How do you remain faithful? How do you live with faith? How do you live without doubt? How do you separate your current situation(s) from your faith?

Day 1: David: Faith Defined
       1 Samuel; 2 Samuel; Psalm

Day 2: Mary: An Exercise of Faith
       Luke 1:26—38

Day 3: Peter: Faith Failed
       Matthew 14:27—33

Day 4: Paul: Faith Re—Birthed
       Acts 9

Day 5: Esther: An Extravagant Faith
       Esther 5

Day One: David—A Faith Defined

1 Samuel; 2 Samuel; Psalm

1 Samuel 16:1 God tells Samuel that He has chosen one of Jesse's sons to be the next king. Samuel is not sure that he wants that assignment. God reassures him. In verse 7, God tells him what He is interested in: his heart; not his appearance. After all of Jesse's sons have appeared before Samuel, Samuel asks Jesse if all of his sons have been here. Jesse confesses that there is still one more, the youngest. When the youngest appears, God selects him. David, age 12, will be king.

When? How? Training? King at 12? Not actually. God plans his training. With Saul. Over a period of years. David could have been impatient about when, as is natural of humans, but he waited until God's appointed time to take the throne, not a moment sooner.

That required faith. Faith: Real, Authentic Faith.

Faith is not easily defined as what it is but is definitely known for what it is not.

1. Would you have been patient like David while waiting to be king?

_____
_____
_____
_____
_____

2. Is God's word, actions good enough for you to have faith in? If so, why and when? If not, why not?

_____
_____
_____
_____
_____

3. Do you have the faith that God can be pleased with? Hebrews 11:6. Why or why not? When will you have that measure of faith?

_____
_____
_____
_____
_____

When I first heard that scripture Hebrews 11:6, "Without faith, it is impossible to please God," I was breathless. I was overwhelmed. I then turned reflective: did I have the faith that would please God? That is not a one—time question. You have to ask that frequently, based on what you are living through at that moment.

David was made king, without having to kill Saul. David won many battles, starting with the battle with Goliath—incredible faith. David accomplished almost all that God said that he would.

David sinned with Bathsheba. From that union, they bore a son. As a consequence, for that sin, the child became ill. During this illness, David fasted and prayed until he discovered that the child died. Faith. When he found out that he died, he bathed, dressed, and went to see Bathsheba. Out of that union, Solomon was born. FAITH.

Many of us would have reacted differently.

4. How would you react when your child is taken? Even if you are the reason for the death?

_____
_____
_____
_____
_____

David continued to love and obey God, even through his trouble, some self—inflicted. David was a man after God's own heart.

5. Why was David given that label? What is required to earn that same label? When will you start that work?

___

David is an example of faith and he also had a period of doubt—a lack of faith. David started to doubt and count what God had done. That offended God. So much so that the punishment was that David would not be able to build the house for the Ark of the Covenant. Further, God offered David three options—all of which penalized the people of Israel for his sins.

6. What have you done that has caused others to be penalized?

___

7. How will you be more faithful?

_____
_____
_____
_____
_____

Bible Study for Women

Day Two: Mary—An Exercise of Faith

Luke 1:26—38

[38] "I am the Lord's servant," Mary answered. "May your word to me be fulfilled." Then the angel left her.

In one afternoon, her life CHANGED! One conversation summoned all of the faith that she had. ALL of it! When the angel visited Mary, her life changed forever. Initially, it did not look well. Was God's favor of Mary enough to survive the possible consequences?

1. What would you have done in Mary's shoes? Are you faithful enough to be chosen for something so significant?

_____
_____
_____
_____
_____

Mary seems so cool, calm and collected. The Bible does not report that she is worried or concerned. It does not share her feelings or thoughts. She visits Elizabeth, but still does not share enough to understand her thoughts and feelings.

2. How would you feel if you were Mary?

_____
_____
_____
_____
_____

Mary has to continue to live with the fact that she is pregnant, and single, although engaged. During a time when they stone a woman to death for this situation. An exercise of faith!

Joseph had to have a similar conversation in order for him to remain on board with the engagement and consequently the marriage. FAITH.

Mary do not exhibit any doubt. She did not question why her.

3. What causes you to question God? What are your questions for God?

_____
_____
_____
_____
_____

4. When have you exercised in complete faith, without a single doubt?

5. How do you feel when you are completely dependent on God?

6. What can we learn from Mary's faith?

There are times when I consider Mary's choice, her responsibility, I wonder what would have happened if Mary had said no.

What if she did not have enough faith to accept this role? What would God do next?

Faith is comparable to car insurance—it is required. There are major consequences if you don't have it. Without mutual faith, God cannot trust you, which means that you don't get any great, extraordinary roles.

7. Why do you doubt God?

_____
_____
_____
_____
_____

8. Have you considered asking God to restore your faith?

_____
_____
_____
_____
_____

Day Three: Peter—Faith Failed

Matthew 14:27—33

[31] Immediately Jesus reached out his hand and caught him. "You of little faith," he said, "why did you doubt?"

Peter had one of the best roles in the Bible. Peter gets to see and experience some remarkable events. Peter has been the first to walk with Jesus. He sits at the table with Jesus learning and listening. So one day after Peter had witnessed Jesus preach and teach to well over 5000 people, Peter challenged Jesus. "If it is You, Jesus, call me out to You." Wow! Peter, is there anything you won't ask? Actually, no.

Jesus invites Peter to walk on water. Peter's challenge was not initially based on faith, but when he lacked the required faith, Jesus challenged him.

Peter walked on water! In front of all of the other disciples.

1. What is your 'walk on water'?

_____
_____
_____
_____
_____

2. Why did Peter get distracted? What can you do to keep from being distracted?

___

3. What would you have done differently than Peter?

___

"Oh you of little faith!" said Jesus.

4. How would those words make you feel? Do you deserve Jesus to say that to you?

___

Bible Study for Women

Peter knew enough to be completely faithful. Peter walked with Jesus through crowds, heard Jesus teach and preach, watched Jesus heal the sick, witnessed the water become wine, and forced Jesus to reattach the ear of a soldier. Just to name a few things.

5. What else does Jesus have to do to prove that He deserves your faith?

6. What do you learn from Peter?

7. Why does Jesus continue to invest in Peter? Us? Especially when our faith has failed?

_____
_____
_____
_____
_____

The example that Peter sets is one that we need to consider the details of our lives so that we can thoroughly examine it for what God and Jesus experience.

Some of our actions, including a lack of faith, surprises God.

8. Why do we stop having faith? What makes us stop having faith? Is it something specific that happens or is it a mystery?

_____
_____
_____
_____
_____

When we fail God, we should repent, apologize, and reset to start again. We should commit to give God our very best selves—the person He created.

9. Is it easy to recognize when you have failed God? If so, how do you find out? David had Nathan. Who do you have?

_____
_____
_____
_____
_____

10. How do you repent, apologize, and reset after you have failed?

_____
_____
_____
_____
_____

When Jesus saved Peter from drowning on the water and walked Peter back to the boat, I wonder what Peter was thinking. I also wonder what Jesus was thinking. Was that walk quiet?

11. What would have you been saying to yourself or to Jesus on the walk back?

_____

A Woman Like Me

Bible Study for Women

Day Four: Paul—Faith Re—Birthed

Acts 9

If you are not Jesus but have the power that Jesus has, then you are likely to strike Saul to death because of what he said about you.

But we are not Jesus and because Saul slandered Jesus and not us, Jesus did not strike him down or sentence him to death. But rather Jesus saw more than we would have or that we do, ever.

Jesus saw beyond Saul's fault and used that 'fault' to transform Saul to Paul and the most prolific author of almost half of the new testament. Jesus uses His gifts of speaking and influence to be a preacher for Jesus.

Acts 9 tells the story of Saul's transformation.

1. Did Jesus pick me in the same manner? How were you chosen?

_____
_____
_____
_____
_____

Saul did not believe in Jesus and was spreading bad information about Jesus everywhere. In Acts 9, Jesus calls Saul out. Jesus blinded Saul on the road to Damascus. In a matter of a few days, Saul was evangelizing and sharing the good news about Jesus.

Faith accompanied the transformation.

2. Do we take action for Jesus with this speed and sense of urgency?

_____
_____
_____
_____
_____

3. Is our transformation of faith this memorable? How so? Describe.

_____
_____
_____
_____
_____

One of Paul's concerns after his transformation was how were people going to respond to him speaking for Jesus, after he had spent so much time speaking against Jesus.

4. Does that sound familiar?

5. Are we more concerned about what others will say about what we do for Jesus than we are trying to please God?

6. How could Jesus be sure that Paul would accept his new assignment? How sure is Jesus when He assigns you a role?

From enemy to friend in about 10 days. Trusted with several books of the New Testament. Traveled throughout the nations to share Jesus and pray, preach, and teach. Imprisoned for Jesus.

7. What does you list consist of?

8. What do we learn from Paul's story?

9. Describe Paul's faith.

Bible Study for Women

_____
_____
_____
_____

Day Five: Esther—An Extravagant Faith
Esther 5

A new queen! The dream of every woman: Queen! Unexpected. Interesting transition. Well, Esther has to be a better queen than the previous queen. She needed faith to audition for Queen, to present herself to the king, and then to become queen.

Esther was not supposed to be there. Her family was not the 'right' religion. When she was made Queen, she was still timid, trying to figure out what her role was and what the limitations are as queen. She has to become acclimated to her surroundings.

While she was getting settled, one of the King's men was trying to hurt her cousin. Mordecai asked Esther to help him. Initially, she seemed hesitant. With some encouragement, she conjured enough courage to speak to the king about the matter.

1. Do you have the courage that Esther had to do the right thing for others?

_____
_____
_____
_____
_____

2. What does it cost us to help others? Why?

___

3. Why do we always ask what is in it for me before we help another individual?

___

4. What is required to stop asking that question?

___

5. Do you admire Esther?

_____
_____
_____
_____
_____

When Esther goes to see the King about the situation with her cousin, he listens and it went differently than she expected.

6. When you have pursued something that you have absolutely been afraid of, what was the outcome? What did your faith bring you?

_____
_____
_____
_____
_____

7. Who has faith that you admire? Why?

_____

8. Who do you share your faith with? How do they respond?

9. Esther taught us several lessons. What were the lessons you learned? What will you share with others that you have learned?

10. Does the amount of risk impact the measure of our faith? Why or why not?

_____
_____
_____
_____

Bible Study for Women

Week Four: Trust

Memory Verse:

¹ In you, LORD my God,
I put my trust.

Psalm 25:1

Trust is an interesting word with 24 definitions and six word constructs: noun, adjective, verb without object, verb with object, verb phrases, and an idiom. Trust is also subjective and relative. Trust is defined as confidence; the reliance on the integrity, strength, ability, surety, etc., of a person or thing. Also, defined as hope. So the word has many contextual meanings.

Trust is also earned. We trust based on many factors which may be intangible and may be unable to explain. This week we will study trust in God. Trust seems intangible, but trust causes some things to happen: trust causes belief, trust reflects love, trust signifies faith, trust summons confidents, and trust casts away fear.

There is an age—old debate about trust being earned rather than given; trust until given a reason to not to trust. These practices apply to other humans, but not to God.

Trust until. Some people don't trust God anymore. Something happened and God didn't answer their prayer the way they wanted, so they don't trust, or lack of faith or don't even believe.

Trust God until. Even after. Why did God do what He did the way He did? We don't know. We may understand one day. It is more likely that we will never know. God's will override our prayers and desires. Trust.

He has the big glasses on.

Trust.

Day 1: Trust in the Lord

    Proverbs 3:5; Psalm 44:6

Day 2: Love and Trust

    1 Corinthians 13:7; Psalm 13:5; Nahum 1:7

Day 3: A Declaration of Trust

    Psalm 25:1; Psalm 119:66

Day 4: A Legacy of Trust

    Psalm 22:4; Psalm 146:3; Proverbs 22:19

Day 5: Beyond All Else: Trust
Psalm 56:11; Isaiah 26:4

Day One: Trust in the Lord

Psalm 44:6

⁶ I put no trust in my bow, my sword does not bring me victory;

Proverbs 3:5

⁵ Trust in the LORD with all your heart and lean not on your own understanding;

Trust in the Lord. Unconditionally. Unwavering. Consistent. Without doubt. Without a worry. Trust. When you consider your level of trust in God, based on 1 being no trust and 10 being totally trust, what is your number? Why?

_____
_____
_____
_____

Trust is something you use daily. You sit on a chair daily that you did not build or even check for the sturdiness or sufficient support. Did you check your chair for all of the screws? Do you check your engine before you leave home in your car? Do you check all of the tires on your vehicle for screws or nails? No, you don't. You sit on that chair without a second thought. You start that car and drive away, trusting that it will deliver you to all of your destinations. You do this daily without a second thought. You sit, drive, and a million other things, including eat food that you did not prepare.

But when someone suggests that you trust in God, you have a million questions, all associated with doubt and scrutiny. You second guess every word, deed, strategy, and action. You cast away those who try to share God with you. And keep in mind, you are a believer with all of this doubt.

1. How did you get here?

___

2. What does God have to do to earn your trust?

___

3. Why is it so hard to trust God?

___

4. What does it look like when you trust God?

5. How can you help others trust in God?

6. How do you feel when you actually trust in God?

7. Did you ever trust God? How do you know that you fully trusted?

8. What happened to make you stop trusting God? When you decided to stop trusting God, was that a good idea?

9. Who do you know that trusts God, though you think that they should not?

Bible Study for Women

10. When we consider the people that we trust, how do those people have your trust but God does not?

11. When we consider your life and the people who you 'trust,' how do they earn and return your trust?

"Trust in the Lord with all your heart."

With all of your heart. Give God your whole heart. Trust only occurs with your whole heart. Partitioning your heart means that you cannot trust God fully. You are not all in. Without all of your heart, you are anticipating failure and feel that is imminent.

Conversely, when you give your whole heart, and you authentically trust God, your trust is not revoked with the slightest issue. When you are all—in, then you are willing and able to forgive God if something does not appear to favor you. Further, when you trust with your whole heart, when something does not appear to favor you, you are willing to wait for the reveal about why this was the best course of action.

12. Does God know that you trust Him? How?

_____
_____
_____
_____
_____

Think about when you have completely trusted God. Return to this place. You need more than ever to trust in God. With your whole heart.

"I put not trust in my bow."

"And lean not on your own understanding."

Both, your bow and whatever fighting element you use, and your understanding can and will fail you. Your bow can mislabel a foe and cause you to fight an advocate. Consider when you have done that and how you felt when you to retreat.

13. Have you ever treated God as the enemy? Why? How did you transform that error?

_____

_____

_____

_____

_____

Your 'understanding' has a slant. It is subjective. It is an opinion. It is ever changing. It is shaped by elements which are not of God. It is fueled and shaped by others who do not have your same relationship with God. Your understanding is unreliable and fleeting.

Don't depend on your inconsistent and ill—prepared understanding in order to decided to not trust God. Do you really think that if you cannot decide what shirt to wear or which boots look best with that shirt that your 'understanding' is reliable enough to decide not to trust in God.

Trust in God.

Day Two: Love and Trust

1 Corinthians 13:7; Psalm 13:5; Nahum 1:7

It would appear that in order to trust, then love must be active. Trust is not authentic without love. Even before you read the verses, you may have known that. Do you trust someone that you don't love? Do you love someone that you don't trust?

Remember that agape love is necessary for every relationship. Love in an investment in the other person. Trust is an investment in the other person.

The love chapter of the Bible: 1 Corinthians outlines the details and definitions of love. It clarifies that love is a verb. Love is demonstrated, not discussed. Love always trusts. Always.

Recall a relationship when you stopped trusting someone that you loved. Did that happen simultaneously? Did one thing happen first? Then the other?

An event or situation causes trust to called into question. If that event or situation has merit—proven true, then the love starts to fade. A total review of the relationship crosses your mind, doubt elevates, and maybe you call the entire relationship into question.

When trust fails, love will soon disappear. How can we demonstrate love to God? Trust. Are they mutually exclusive: can one exist without the other? Are the mutually dependent: can they exist without each other?

So it is with God. Can you say that you love God, but do not trust Him? How is that possible? If you say that you love Him, then it means that you should also trust Him.

I was supposed to be a successful Financial Planner. I was studying to pass the Series 7 and Series 66 exams. I was at a major firm and was on the road to success, finally directly using this expensive undergraduate degree. I had been a retail manager. I was looking forward to this new career. I went to take the test and failed the exam. By 1 point. I don't fail tests. I am a very successful student. As a result of failing the test, I was no longer employed with the firm. So at that very moment, I was temporarily unemployed. I called a district manager who extended me a job over the phone. Fast forward nine months later, I was asleep on the sofa at home when a plane crashed into the World Trade Center in New York. Hundreds of people died in those terroristic actions. The fact of the matter was that I would have been in that building if I had passed that test.

I had to trust God would let me fail because He did not plan for me in that building. I was taught to trust God. I am very persistent so it was surprising that I complied with this process.

Lord, if it be Your will. . . . That means that I trust His will.

Nahum reads, "He cares for those who trust Him." The obvious conclusion is that He does not care for those who do not trust Him. I cannot validate that, however He has stated that if we trust Him, then He will care for us. I need Him to care for me and care about me.

David speaks in Psalm 13: "But I trust in Your unfailing love; my heart rejoices in Your salvation." The key word is unfailing. His love is unfailing.

1. David has lots of proof. What proof do you have of His unfailing love? Do you share that?

   _____
   _____
   _____
   _____
   _____

2. What has to happen for you to completely trust God?

   _____
   _____
   _____
   _____
   _____

3. Is it hard to love? Is it hard to trust? Why or why not?

   _____
   _____
   _____
   _____
   _____

4. Can love and trust be taught? If not, how does it happen?

___

5. Is it riskier to trust God or to not trust Him?

Day Three: A Declaration of Trust

Psalm 25:1 (NIV)

¹ In you, LORD my God,

   I put my trust.

Psalm 119:66

The King James version of Psalm 25:1 reads: "In Thee Oh Lord, I put my trust."

This is my favorite version of this scripture. The New International Version seems a little softer in its firmness to declare the trust David has for God.

This declaration of trust is what God is looking for from us. Will we declare that we are all in and that we are totally surrendered to God? Total surrender to God is a declaration of trust.

1. Can you surrender to God? Is it hard to surrender? If so, why? If not, why not?

_____
_____
_____
_____
_____

Bible Study for Women

2. If you do not plan/want/able to trust and surrender, then why do you ask God for anything?

_____
_____
_____
_____
_____

3. Have you ever had someone totally dependent on you but they were not willing to surrender to you? Has ever happened to you? How did that make you feel? What happened when that continued?

_____
_____
_____
_____
_____

4. A Declaration of Trust. Required. All—in. Demonstrative. Decisive. Unwavering. Can you? Will you?

_____
_____
_____

Psalm 119:66 reads, "Teach me knowledge and good judgement, for I trust Your commands." The only person who we learn from is someone we trust. If you are going to learn knowledge and good judgment, then it should be from God. He is the seer of all things and the knower of all things. He is also the giver of wisdom.

5. What is your capacity for knowledge? For good and sound judgement? For wisdom? How did you determine that capacity?

6. What is your capacity to trust? How did you decide that?

7. Are you in good mental and emotional state so that you can learn? Receive wisdom? Be able to trust?

_____
_____
_____
_____
_____

It is time to offer a Declaration of Trust.

Day Four: A Legacy of Trust

Psalm 146:3

³ Do not put your trust in princes,
   in human beings, who cannot save.

"In You, our ancestors put their trust; they trusted and You delivered them." Psalm 22:4

Proverbs 22:19

When you considered 'ancestors,' these are people before you—relatives, parents, elders, people you trust whom you follow regardless of what they say. Legacy is what your family does and you follow what same path.

There are legacies in colleges, jobs and in social organizations. This means that the new member already has a connection. It is not outwardly spoken that there is automatic acceptance and admittance. In some instances, it has the total opposite effect. But with God, legacy is the best thing ever. You are already familiar with God, His deeds, and His reputation. You should not have to be convinced that God is God. You should not need any proof that God should be trusted. You should not need to be convinced that God is worth trusting.

In 2 Timothy 1:5, it refers to the faith of Timothy's grandmother and mother, 'now lives in you also.' This is a legacy of faith. Likewise, you are first introduced to most things at home. You learned to walk, talk, eat, and play at home. It is socially expected that you will use those skills in the public and everywhere you trod.

Legacy is built at home. You will need to trust, demonstrate trust, and teach others to trust. The legacy that you leave for your family and other people who watch your every move.

Legacy is the proper way to share information and wealth, influence and power. In the work place, it is called nepotism and it is frowned upon because there seems to be an unfair advantage.

However, with God there is not unfair advantage. God treats legacy and new Christians the same. The legacy is helpful to assist with the learning needs of others.

1. Are you a legacy or non—legacy? Does it matter?

___

2. What are the responsibilities of those who would be labeled legacy? Is this difficult?

___

Day Five: Above and Beyond All Else: Trust

Psalm 56:11

"In God I trust and am not afraid.

What can man do to me?" Psalm 56:11

Isaiah 26:4

'In God we Trust' are very familiar words. That statement is on the back of all US currency. In fact, I also saw it on the back of a police SUV the other day. But do we mean those words all the time? Do we know what it means to uphold those words at all times? In many instances, we forget and/or take those words for granted.

How do we trust above all else?

Here are a few suggestions:

1. Trust because doubt is easier. Philippians 4:6
2. Trust because God while He may have 'failed' you, according to your definition and desires, He has not left you or forsaken you. Romans 8:28
3. Trust because He promised blessings. Psalm 40:4; Jeremiah 17:7
4. Trust because He gives you the work to do. Psalm 37:5
5. Trust because all others and all other things have actually failed you. Psalm 20:7; Psalm 118:8—9
6. Trust in the Lord because not trusting is disobedience. Psalm 9:10; Isaiah 26:4
7. Trust in the Lord because He is your refuge. Psalm 62:8; Psalm 86:2
8. Trust in God because you will be well. Psalm 28:7
9. Trust in God because He is for us. Romans 8:31
10. Trust in God because He loves us. Romans 8:37—39; John 3:16; Ephesians 3:14—21

11. Trust in God because we will not be separated from God. Romans 8:35
12. Trust in God because He forgives you. Psalm 103:3
13. Trust in God because He heals. Psalm 147::3
14. Trust in God because He cares for those who trust Him. 1 Peter 4:7
15. Trust in God because His trust offers His peace. Philippians 4:7

1. What is the most important of these statements? Why?

_____
_____
_____
_____
_____

2. Who will you share these with? Why? How?

_____
_____
_____
_____
_____

3. Can you trust God for your life? What will you do when it is difficult to trust?

_____
_____
_____
_____
_____

Bible Study for Women

Week 5: Prayer

Memory Verse:

[20] Now to him who is able to do immeasurably more than all we ask or imagine, according to his power that is at work within us, [21] to him be glory in the church and in Christ Jesus throughout all generations, for ever and ever! Amen.

Ephesians 3:20—21

When I kneel before the Father to pray, I am barely audible to others. Prayer is about relationship with God.

Prayer is an intimate conversation between you and God. There is not a prescription to the proper way to pray. Just talk to God. It's not the same for everyone nor every time you pray.

There are some people who are perceived to be some of the most powerful prayer warriors ever. They pray. God listens. God delivers. It seems that God never says no to them. What these prayer warriors do know is that they can talk to God at any time, so they do. When they talk to God, they humbly go before our Father and honestly confess their desires, their sins, ask for forgiveness and praise, adore, and thank God for all that He is and everything He does.

Prayer is a time to commune with God in the most honest and intimate conversation you will have everyday.

Prayer refreshes our soul and calms our spirit. Prayer requires honesty and humility, depth and love, perseverance and persistence. Prayer forces you to leave your burdens at god's alter and leave them there forever.

The most important part is honesty.

The second part is intercessory prayer; praying for others. Putting the needs of others before your own. Pray.

Day 1: Some Notes about Prayer

        1 Thessalonians 5:17

Day 2: The Authors of Prayer

        Matthew 6:9—13

Day 3: One of My Favorite Prayers

        Ephesians 3:14—21

Day 4: The Assignment of Intercession

        John 17

Day 5: In Jesus' Name, I pray. Amen.
John 14:13—14

Day One: Some Notes about Prayer

1 Thessalonians 5:17

Pray continually.

The petition of God happens while in prayer. God awaits to hear from you. He anticipates your prayer more than you fear the interaction. The best aspect about prayer is that there is no script for prayer. God wants to hear from your heart. He may need to correct it but He wants to hear from you.
There are instructions about prayer and some suggestions about prayer.

Matthew 6:6 advises that you go into a secret place to pray so that you and God can commune. This verse also offers that you will be rewarded for praying. Prayer is better than talking to your best friend, so I have not been influenced by the reward. I cannot confirm what that reward is, but I do know that I feel better.

1 Thessalonians 5:17 reads, 'pray continually.' Pray all the time about everything. Everything? Yes, everything.

When you pray, you also need to be sensitive to the answer.

Jesus taught us how to pray in Matthew 6:9—13. He offered some suggestions based on the shabby prayers that He witnessed. He leads this suggestion with do not sound like the hypocrites, which also means don't be a hypocrite, and don't pray to be seen. Prayer is not for building social status. Prayer does not take a long time either. Matthew 6:5—15.

1. Do you pray? How often? What do you pray for?

_____
_____
_____
_____
_____

When you pray, fasting comes up. Fasting is a time when you deprive yourself something(s) that is separating you from God. This period of fasting is designed to move you closer to God. Also, fasting is used to find answers, which you have posed to God in prayer. Matthew 6:16—18. Fasting is done in secret unless you have a fasting partner or a spouse.

2. Have you ever fasted? What happened? Do you fast regularly?

_____
_____
_____
_____
_____

Prayer is based on relationship. Matthew 18:19 promotes praying with others and they agree about what they ask for, their request will be granted, in accordance to God's will.

Prayer is based on relationship. John 15:7 reads, "If you remain in Me (Jesus) and My words remain in you, ask whatever you wish, and it will be done for you." John 15 teaches a great message—John 15:1—17. God is the gardener. Jesus is the vine. We are the branches. We are the product of the time we spend with Jesus. Prayer is a part of that time.

3. What is your relationship with God and Jesus like? Is it the first thing that you take care of or does it come as an afterthought? Why?

_____
_____
_____
_____
_____

4. What can you do to become closer to God?

_____
_____
_____
_____
_____

5. What prevents you from praying?

___

6. What causes you to pray?

___

7. Who is your example of prayer?

___

8. Who helped you define prayer? How did that happen?

_____
_____
_____
_____
_____

Day Two: The Authors of Prayer

Matthew 6:9—13

⁹ "This, then, is how you should pray:

"'Our Father in heaven,

hallowed be your name,

¹⁰ your kingdom come,

your will be done,

   on earth as it is in heaven.

¹¹ Give us today our daily bread.

¹² And forgive us our debts,

   as we also have forgiven our debtors.

¹³ And lead us not into temptation,

   but deliver us from the evil one.'

God is the Author of prayer. God prescribes prayer for communication with Him. Prayer is not easy or comfortable. Prayer requires focus, honesty, transparency, hope, and faith. A conversation with God requires stamina. He does not always answer immediately, nor does He give you all of your requests. He may seem to be ignoring you altogether.

God will consider your attitude and motives when you present your petition to God. 'What will fulfilling this request do for your future and your relationship with God?' That is His question when He decides about your request. He also considers 'How does this factor into and fulfill His will?' If this does not advance His will, then the answer is likely to be no.

The act of prayer is not a perfunctory measure, but rather a reverent manner so that you will respect the relationship between the two of you.

God has allowed us to prayer in all conditions and circumstances.

When God gifted us with Jesus. Jesus took prayer to the next level by teaching us to pray, Matthew 6:5—15. He taught fasting in Matthew 6:16—18.

1. When did you start to pray?

   _____
   _____
   _____
   _____
   _____

2. What do you pray about?

   _____
   _____
   _____
   _____
   _____

3. How do you share what you know about prayer?

_____
_____
_____
_____

Prayer is a standard of excellence between you and God and Jesus. Prayer was designed for you to share your whole heart with Jesus and God.

Prayer is a conference between You and God. God did not have to extend this to us. He does not have to listen to us. Being sovereign means that He is absolute. Final. Comprehensive.

When Jesus teaches prayer, He does so because He knows that we don't have any idea about what our prayer voice means, what that voice affords us, and what me do to God when we pray.

Prayer warriors are sent by God, anointed by God to His assigned work.

There are some specific people who are gifted with that role. We will discuss three of them briefly. Paul, David, and Mary.

Mary is known is one of the famous moms in the world She birthed Jesus! At some point though, she had to also understand that she had birthed her own Savior. That will make you pray. She shares with us the power of prayer without needing to exercise her role as His mom. She prayed that she will understand her role and be able to honor God by doing well the role for which she was chosen. Luke 1. Mary's prayers also teach us to worship. Her behavior cause others to complain. Luke 10:38—42.

David is a warrior: prayer and physical. He fought the enemies with stones and spears, but he also fought those some enemies on his knees in prayer. My favorite prayer was after his sinful behavior, 2 Samuel 12:15—25. He sinned. He confessed. He repented. He prayed and fasted. He admitted and acknowledged God. He was punished and forgiven. He taught his servants a valuable lesson (v. 22—23). He was the king and he still prayed to God who he had sinned against, who had designated him as king. He still prayed.

Paul! The person who was transformed by being summoned by Jesus, then questioned by Jesus. Paul could not answer Jesus, so he submitted to Jesus.

When Paul authored half of New Testament, he opens and/or close each book with prayer. He prays for others and he intercedes for us because he submitted to his role.

Paul prays some powerful prayers. It is not a credit to Paul. The prayer came from God. The fact that Paul did not stifle the prayers that God sends to him affirms that prayer is the gift, the anointing.

Paul has blessed us so much through his obedience.

Consider Philippians 1:3—5, [3]I thank My God every time I remember you. [4] In all my prayers for all of you, I always pray with joy [5] because of your partnership in the gospel from the first day until now. . .

This prayer is just one of many which should move you and influence you to further understand the power of prayer.

1. Describe your prayer life as it compares to Mary's. What can you do to improve your prayer life?

___

2. Explain your understanding of David's prayer life. Would you haave been as honest when repenting and confessing to Nathan about your sins?

___

3. Share your perspective about David's lesson to his staff about why it was acceptable to stop praying and fasting.

___

Bible Study for Women

_____
_____
_____
_____

4. Paul prays for everyone. What does Paul teach you about intercessory prayer?

_____
_____
_____
_____

5. When will you pray?

_____
_____
_____

6. Time?

_____
_____

7. Prayer partner(s):

8. Prayer concern(s):

Bible Study for Women

Day Three: One of my Favorite Prayers

Ephesians 3:14—21

A Prayer for the Ephesians

[14] For this reason I kneel before the Father, [15] from whom every family in heaven and on earth derives its name. [16] I pray that out of his glorious riches he may strengthen you with power through his Spirit in your inner being, [17] so that Christ may dwell in your hearts through faith. And I pray that you, being rooted and established in love, [18] may have power, together with all the Lord's holy people, to grasp how wide and long and high and deep is the love of Christ, [19] and to know this love that surpasses knowledge—that you may be filled to the measure of all the fullness of God.
[20] Now to him who is able to do immeasurably more than all we ask or imagine, according to his power that is at work within us, [21] to him be glory in the church and in Christ Jesus throughout all generations, for ever and ever! Amen.

Of all of the prayers written in the Bible, this one is my absolute favorite. No matter what I am doing, I am moved to tears when I read it or when I hear it read.

Why is it so significant? Well, let's study the verses together.

Verses 14 and 15. Paul announces that he is about to pray and that He is praying to the God of everybody. That statement prepares you for that best prayer after the Lord's prayer.

Verse 16. Paul does not hesitate to ask God to strengthen me out of His glorious riches with power. Power for my inner being! Paul prays for the strength of my inner being! Who prays for your inner strength and power? You don't even pray for your own self with that kind of request!

Verse 17. Verse 17 finishes verse 16 with so that Christ may dwell in your hearts with faith. This declaration means that the power is not real without faith. Your inner being needs to be strong in order to possess the power of Christ, house to Spirit of the Lord, and use that power to carry out the will of God.

The second part of verse 17 declares that I am "rooted and established in love." This removes all doubt that love and being of value, enhancing self—esteem and overall self—worth. I was made with love from the very Definition of Love.

1. There are certain words when strung together should uplift you. There are some of those words. How does that make you feel?

___

Verse 18 offers me power, and all God's people, to understand the measure of God's love. Paul prays that I have enough power to understand God's love. God's love is so comprehensive that I need power to understand! The measure of God's love is wide, high, deep, and long. As a math teacher, I define that as infinity. Area is calculated by length and width. Volume is calculated by length, width, and height. But then there is depth. The word depth indicates that the love penetrates the surface—our surfaces—to reach the unseen places of our minds and hearts so that God can help us recover from what hurts us. God's love is infinite. We need power to understand and to accept His love.

2. In what ways do you reject God's love for you?

___

_____
_____
_____
_____

3. What does that measurement mean to you?

_____
_____
_____
_____

4. Did that measurement move you emotionally? I cry every time.

_____
_____
_____
_____

Verse 19. Paul then shares that this love sometimes does not make ANY sense. He loves you when you would not even love yourself. You don't understand why He loves you or why He still loves you when you have done _____ ; whatever you fill that blank with. You will want to dismiss it and reject it; undermine it and confuse it. God's love is not always explainable not reasonable; which is why it is God's love, rather than our love.

5. How can you better accept God's love?

_____

_____

_____

_____

_____

Verse 20 and 21. Paul worships God by declaring that His omnipresence and omnipotence is at work with us according to our self—imposed limitations, and offers His our glory and honor.

Whew! Paul prayed for seven verses which makes me cry upon the consideration of those words.

6. Summarize the verses for yourself and what will you share with others.

_____

_____

_____

_____

7. Did these verses help you understand how much power prayers have? Explain.

_____
_____
_____
_____
_____

Bible Study for Women

Day Four: The Assignment of Power—Intercession

John 17

¹After Jesus said this, He looked toward heaven and prayed:

"Father, the hour has come. Glorify Your Son, that Your Son may glorify you.

When you read John 17, have a handkerchief nearby. Jesus prays for us fervently. At a level which makes my heart flutter and feel guilty that I don't pray that way.

In the first five verses, Jesus prays for Himself. These five verses are comprehensive, and sacrificial. Jesus commits His life to God and reminds God of what He has done.

1. Describes how this makes you feel. Did you have any questions about His prayer?

_____

_____

_____

_____

_____

In the next 14 verses, Jesus prayed for His disciples—the ones who walked closely with Him. The prayers that He utters to God is so profound! Jesus edifies them to God. He praises their behavior. He promotes their obedience. He asks for their protection. He admits His feelings and fears. He even mentions—prays for—the one who betrayed Him, forgiving him because scripture is never false.

2. If you were His disciple, how would His prayer make you feel? What would you say in response?

_____
_____
_____
_____

In the final seven (7) scriptures, Jesus prayers for all of us as believers. The second sentence of verse 20 states that, I pray for those who will believe in Me through their message! That was so powerful! It made me blush and I was immediately humbled.

Further, Jesus teaches during prayer as well. Selflessness. Compassion. Love. Forgiveness. Protection. Purpose. Future. Salvation. Mission. Promise.

Read those words aloud. Slowly. Remembering that He is talking about you.

3. How does that prayer make you feel? What does that mean to you?

_____
_____
_____
_____

For everything that we are asked to do, Jesus did it first. Obviously, prayer is a command based on relationship. He prayed to God, His Father, who could already read His thoughts and does not actually need to pray. However, prayer is based on relationship and a discipline. Discipline is required to pray. The discipline is not for the prayer, but for the results. When you pray, you have been putting God on the 'clock.'

'By Friday' is my reference to my due dates for people and projects. There are times when that due date is an actual expectation. I have imposed that deadline of this Friday even it is Thursday, the day before. I have done this in my retail career, my family, my relationships. And also, I have done it to God. Whether it is realistic or not, I have imposed this deadline and when it is not met, there are consequences.

But I gave that deadline to God. I have no control over what God does and when God does anything or if He will respond, but I still want what I asked for when I asked for it. Not in a little while. Not in time. Not in God's time. Not when it is appropriate. Not when I am mature enough or knowledgeable enough.

4. How will you manage the wait time associated with praying to God?

_____

_____

_____

_____

_____

The second part is the honesty during prayer. God is not to be treated like your best friend. He is God. The discipline of your prayer relationship will falter if you are not honest.

5. How will you commit to be HONEST with God? Why haven't you been honest with God previously?

_____
_____
_____
_____
_____

The third part is the gift of intercession. As we intercede for others, we witnessed Him do that first. So likewise, we need to intercede for others—with or without their request. He teaches intercession as well as demonstrating a life filled with prayer.

6. Who are we supposed to be praying for? Do you pray for others? How do you determine for whom to pray?

_____
_____
_____
_____
_____

Bible Study for Women

7. Who prays for you? Were you honest when you asked for prayer?

_____

_____

_____

_____

_____

8. What are you praying for right now? Who have you shared this list with?

_____

_____

_____

_____

_____

The issue with intercessory prayer is trust. People do not share with you what they are praying about, which is very personal to them, if they don't think that they can trust you. Be careful when you are talking to other people about other people, which is gossip, because people are judging your walk by that very context of that conversation.

Imagine how you feel about people who shared what you trusted them with.

9. Do you have the trust necessary for others to ask for prayer?

10. Reflect on the total chapter. What will you share with others? What will you change about your prayer life? Who will know/notice? How will you influence the life of others because of your prayer life?

Day Five: In Jesus' Name, I Pray. Amen.

John 14:13—14; 15:16; 16:23, 26

¹³ And I will do whatever you ask in my name, so that the Father may be glorified in the Son. ¹⁴ You may ask me for anything in my name, and I will do it.

In this social media climate and network based on advancement, name dropping is a focus. Who do you know? Who you know makes a difference in your life. Knowing the right person gets you a job or a house or a ticket to see your favorite musician or sports team. Name dropping is popular and an easy tool to use to get things done for yourself.

This establishes a status and then it's your name that people want to start dropping to help them with areas of their lives.

Name dropping is so much more powerful when that person does the name dropping. When I call the person which can help you directly and edify and recommend you, that goes further than you calling someone and saying I said to call or it was okay to use my name.

When Jesus offers the use of His name, that is the ultimate in name dropping! John 14:13—14 shares that Jesus will do whatever I ask in His name so that God will be glorified. Because I ask in His name, He will grant it. My request still has to be granted according to His will. That is the ultimate is name dropping. In Jesus' name, I pray and ask for all of these blessings. I pray that God and Jesus honor my requests so that I can be productive for Their glory and in Their service.

1. What have you asked for in Jesus' name? What was the outcome of the request?

   _____
   _____
   _____
   _____
   _____

2. Did you know the power of asking in the name of Jesus? How will use His name differently now that you know?

   _____
   _____
   _____
   _____
   _____

3. Why would Jesus extend Him name for our use?

   _____
   _____
   _____
   _____
   _____

John 15:16, "You did not choose Me, but I chose you and appointed you go that you might so and bear fruit—fruit that will last—and so that whatever you ask in my name the Father will give you."

He chose me and gave me access to His name! That is a blessing!

Write a prayer, asking for those requests in Jesus' name.

Amen.

Bible Study for Women

Week Six: Wisdom

Memory Verse

[20] You intended to harm me, but God intended it for good to accomplish what is now being done, the saving of many lives.

Genesis 50:20

Wisdom is a tricky concept. Wisdom was most noted with Solomon, David's son. Solomon is a man with an incredible story. Solomon is the son of Bathsheba and David. He is the son born after their son who died which was the product of their adulterous relationship. So for Solomon to be wise is a gift and proof of God's forgiveness.

Proverbs also gives words of wisdom. Wisdom seems distant, also seems for old people. Wisdom should have been developed while growing from experience.

Experience is equated to learning. Learning begets wisdom. Wisdom is demonstrated through decision making and behavior. Wisdom should increase with each experience and each monumental event. In this century, we pray that age and wisdom would be concurrent, however that is not always the case.

Wisdom also while not easy to define or see; it is definitely easy to spot when it is lacking. As we consider who is wise: Solomon, Paul, Elizabeth, Samuel, Joseph, and Proverbs review. Wisdom is enjoyable, but be wary of wisdom—envy. Don't do it. Just ask for it. God promises to grant wisdom to all who ask for it. Wisdom does not allow the misuse of wisdom. When do you decide to ask for wisdom?

What happens when you know you have wisdom? How do you know that you are wise? When do you share your wisdom with others? What does it cost you to be wise? Do people distance themselves because you are wise?

Use your wisdom wisely.

Day 1: Solomon and a Proverbs Review

    1 Kings 3:7—15. Proverbs.

Day 2: Samuel

    1 Samuel

Day 3: Paul

    Acts 9, 10; Romans, Ephesians

Day 4: Elizabeth vs. Zechariah

    Luke 1:1—25

Day 5: Joseph

       Genesis 50:19—20; 47—49

Day One: Solomon and His Wisdom

1 Kings 3:7—15. Proverbs.

⁷ "Now, LORD my God, you have made your servant king in place of my father David. But I am only a little child and do not know how to carry out my duties. ⁸ Your servant is here among the people you have chosen, a great people, too numerous to count or number. ⁹ So give your servant a discerning heart to govern your people and to distinguish between right and wrong. For who is able to govern this great people of yours?"

Solomon is the son of David and Bathsheba, their blessing after they were punished for their initial relational sin. Why is that important? Because the forgiving God we serve, blessed the couple after they had sinned and pled to God for forgiveness. So not only were they forgiven, they were immensely blessed.

Solomon became King at the appointment of his father. God affirmed that appointment when God heard Solomon pray for wisdom.

So in the first two chapters of Kings, there is some turmoil and confusion, resulting in a premature, presumption of who was actually going to assume the throne and a misunderstanding about a woman. After these two issues were resolved, Solomon settles in as king and goes before the Lord in prayer. This prayer has been marked as profound and is labeled the prayer for wisdom, because that is exactly what Solomon asked for. God noted that even He was impressed by what Solomon asked for by granting him wisdom but also granting what he did <u>not</u> ask for: everything else.

Wisdom is accompanied by trust and maturity.

1. If you were appointed 'king,' what would you have prayed for?

___

My guess is that wisdom was not on the initial list. Based on what Solomon demonstrates, it should be the only blessing for which we ask.

2. Does God trust you? Why and why not? What does He trust you? How do you know that God trust's you?

___

3. Solomon was not expecting that bounty. What do you think he told his father, the former king? What would you share if you were him?

4. The definition of wisdom is hard to articulate. What is your definition? How do you share wisdom and its definition with others?

5. How do you teach wisdom to your children? How do you think David taught Solomon wisdom? Or did he?

6. What else did you learn from Solomon during that prayer and God's response to him?

_____
_____
_____
_____
_____

The 31 chapters of Proverbs were authored by Solomon. Several chapters are my favorite. As a woman, Proverbs 31 is the first one. If I had to have a few favorite verses, the following are they: Proverbs 31:10—31, 3:1—7, 12:5; 4:23; 16:9; and 12:25.

Solomon shares wisdom verse after verse, page after page. Proverbs 22 has some popular and widely repeated verses: 22:1, 6; to name two. Further, Proverbs 25:21—22 is known.

7. Which are you favorite three (3) proverbs and why?

   a. _____

_____
_____
_____
_____

b. _____

c. _____

Solomon has been trusted with the throne and the author of Proverbs.

8. What will you do with wisdom that God gifted you with?

A Woman Like Me

Day Two: Samuel

1 Samuel

Hannah is the mother of Samuel who prayed for him, fervently! When Samuel was born, he was the blessing that she prayed for—daily.

Samuel belonged to God before he was born. He was taken to the church at three years old. Hannah promised God that she would deliver Samuel to Him as soon as He was weaned. God was speaking to Samuel at quite a young age: three (3) years old.

Samuel also learned some lessons directly from God. Growing up at the hand of Elijah was hard work. One of the most notable and memorable moments was when God first called Samuel out of his sleep. Samuel woke up Elijah three times until Elijah realized that it was God.

1 Samuel 3:7 reads: 'Now Samuel did not yet know the Lord. The word of the Lord had not been revealed to him.'

In verse 10, the Lord invests and equips Samuel with the details of Eli's punishment. Samuel is trusted and wise, by God's own gifts and definition. Israel's communication with God is channeled through Samuel. Israel asks for a king (1 Samuel 8). They convinced God for a king but that was never God's plan. When God consented, He had Samuel to appoint Saul, the Benjamite He selected (1 Samuel 9 and 10). Although God selected, anointed and appointed Saul, at some point, Saul offended God and would be replaced (1 Samuel 13, 15).

It was Samuel's job to anoint the new king and release the current king (1 Samuel 16).

Wisdom and a relationship with God require listening and perseverance.

1 Samuel 16:7 shares very important life lesson guidelines. Ignore the appearance of the outside—focus on the heart. That is a lifelong lesson which should be applied to all persons at all times.

1. What did you do the first time you heard God speak to you? What would you have done if you were Samuel?

_____
_____
_____
_____
_____

2. Are you surprised that this was Samuel's first direct encounter with God? Why or why not?

_____
_____
_____
_____
_____

Consider the interaction between Samuel and Jesse. Samuel has been assigned to visit and anoint the next king over all of Israel. Samuel stands there while he meets each son. The Lord teaches him patience and wisdom at that very event.

The outcome was David, described as a rudy—faced, lamb attendant, who was twelve (12) years of age. Can you imagine what Samuel was thinking? 'I have stood here all day to anoint a 12-year-old. What is God thinking and what is He doing?'

Samuel was not expecting to pick a replacement that was not immediate. David was 12 and had no idea where this visit would take his life. Neither did Samuel.

Wisdom kept Samuel focused on God and His voice and His directions. Samuel recognized that Saul had fallen short of expectations. Samuel is wise.

3. Based on what you have read, and heard, what have you learned from Samuel? What will you do with that information?

_____
_____
_____
_____
_____

4. If you were Samuel, would you be wondering why you were not selected as King of Israel?

_____
_____
_____
_____
_____

Bible Study for Women

Day Three: Paul

Acts 9 and 10

1. How does Paul, formerly Saul, define wisdom?

_____
_____
_____
_____
_____

Acts 9 chronicles Saul's transition to Paul, the newly called preacher for Christ. Paul is one of my favorite men in the Bible for several reasons. Paul hard to be wise enough to submit to Jesus' calling. Paul (Saul) also had to understand how to be quiet when Jesus asks 'why do you speak against Me?'

Paul became a preacher, a great one, who authored a significant part of the New Testament: Romans, 1 & 2 Corinthians, Galatians, Ephesians, Philippians, Colossians, 1 & 2 Thessalonians, 1 & 2 Timothy, Titus, and Philemon.

2. Would wisdom be a reason why Jesus could call and trust Saul/Paul even though he had been publicly speaking against Jesus? Why did Jesus choose Saul?

_____
_____

_____

_____

Romans: Declares his role and delegation to all of humanity. Romans 1:11-17.

1 Corinthians 13: Paul shared love and the wisdom of adulthood and Christian maturity. Paul supports the definition of love in all ways possible.

2 Corinthians: Paul's transparency in 2 Corinthians 6:3—13 sharing his commitment.

Galatians: Paul shares the fruit of the spirit. 5:23—24

Ephesians: Paul prays and shares love with us in a major way 3:14—21

Philippians: Paul declares that his hardships assist us with serving God. 1:12—14, 16

Colossians: Paul gives spiritual advice and offers Paul's instructions where wisdom certainly resides 3:2—25

1 Thessalonians: Paul is always teaching, which he had to learn and use first, before sharing. 5:12—24

2 Thessalonians: Paul shares profound directions and prayer. 3:5

1 Timothy: Paul mentors Timothy, teaching him how to worship and the criteria for leaders.

2 Timothy: Paul passes the proverbial baton. 3:10—17

Titus: Paul encourages good and shuns others. Titus 1.

Philemon: Paul extends his hand and himself. 1:17

3. Of what you know, and love about Paul, what is the best act he does?

_____

_____

_____

Bible Study for Women

_____
_____

4. Do you consider him as wise? Why or why not?

_____
_____
_____
_____
_____

5. Would you have considered yourself as someone who could have been Paul? What can God choose you to do?

_____
_____
_____
_____
_____

6. What has Paul taught you?

_____

7. As you consider Acts 9 and 10, what have you learned from Saul/Paul?

Bible Study for Women

Day Four: Elizabeth vs. Zechariah

Luke 1:1—25

[18] Zechariah asked the angel, "How can I be sure of this? I am an old man and my wife is well along in years."
[19] The angel said to him, "I am Gabriel. I stand in the presence of God, and I have been sent to speak to you and to tell you this good news. [20] And now you will be silent and not able to speak until the day this happens, because you did not believe my words, which will come true at their appointed time."
[21] Meanwhile, the people were waiting for Zechariah and wondering why he stayed so long in the temple. [22] When he came out, he could not speak to them. They realized he had seen a vision in the temple, for he kept making signs to them but remained unable to speak.

Elizabeth had been barren her entire life. She craved a child but because God did not see fit to bless her all of these years, she had become content and had resolved to not be concerned about it any longer. Zechariah was off at war and was told that Elizabeth would become pregnant. Zechariah questioned Gabriel—in a very disrespectful manner (verse 18). The angel defended his position, but also caused Zechariah not to speak until their son's birth. Now, Zechariah cannot share verbally what he knows. When he returns home, Elizabeth becomes pregnant and says that, "God has done this for me."

She was a wise woman. She was respected in the community. She is unexpectedly, well beyond her years, pregnant.

But now, God has answered a VERY OLD PRAYER.

1. Does that mean that prayers do not have an expiration date? What does that mean in your life? What are some 'old' prayers in your life that you would be surprised if God ever answered in your favor?

___

2. Do you wonder why Gabriel did not tell Elizabeth? Does it seem like Elizabeth had more faith? Was it a test of Zechariah's maturity? Wisdom? Growth?

___

I titled this Elizabeth vs. Zechariah because of the differences between the two. Zechariah thought he was asking a natural question but in fact Gabriel thought he lacked faith. Belief matters when we pray. When we ask God to make mighty moves in our lives, we have to BELIEVE that He can do what we ask. We also have to believe that He will do it when we pray.

3. Is that your story? Do you have disbelief when you pray? If so, when? Why?

4. What did you learn from Elizabeth?

5. What did you learn from Zechariah?

6. Which of them do you share the most in common? Elizabeth vs. Zechariah? Why?

___

This couple gave birth to the man that prepared the way for Jesus. This couple was important to the work of God.

7. Do you think wisdom is expected when you are part of God's word and His will? How would you have done it differently?

___

Bible Study for Women

Day Five: Joseph

Genesis 50:19—20, 37—49

[20] You intended to harm me, but God intended it for good to accomplish what is now being done, the saving of many lives.

Joseph was the next to the youngest of Jacob's twelve sons, and by far the most zealous. He was just excited that had the colorful coat as a gift from Jacob, his dad, which meant, in the eyes of his brothers, that he was his dad's favorite. They did not like that Joseph was the favorite so they planned his demise (Genesis 37). After the coat situation, there was the dream moment, that was the ultimate in their hate rising.

The brothers agreed not to kill him, but to sell him. Reuben was going to secretly return him to his father. They did sell him and made it appear that he was dead by staining the coat.

1. On a scale of 1 to 10, how much wisdom did 17-year-old Joseph have? How much wisdom did you have at 17? What were the consequences for that lack of wisdom?

_____
_____
_____
_____
_____

Joseph is now is Egypt—the new land. While there, he encounters a lot of trouble, but the Lord is with him and gives him favor wherever he goes (Genesis 39) even when the wife is angry that he won't sleep with her and he is put in prison. After another series of events, Joseph is brought out of prison to interpret the King's dreams (Genesis 41) and Joseph gives credit to God.

This leads to Joseph being permanently released from prison. Pharaoh discerned that Joseph was wise and discerning. Pharaoh placed Joseph in charge of all of Egypt. He is now 30 years of age. It has been 13 years since he has last seen his family and in those 13 years, the wisdom he has gained has been monumental.

Genesis 41:50—52, Joseph names his sons based on what God has done for him and through him.

2. In a span of any measure of 13 years, what situations, circumstances, and prayers, have made you wise?

_____
_____
_____
_____
_____

3. How has Joseph's story blessed you so far?

_____

_____

_____

_____

_____

The famine that Pharaoh dreamed about, which Joseph interpreted happened. Joseph was placed in charge and part of what he did was store up food in preparation for the severe famine, which was far—reaching, all the way to his father's house (Genesis 41).

Jacob sent his remaining sons to Egypt for food (Genesis 42). Joseph recognizes them but they do not recognize Joseph. Joseph does not see Benjamin, so he makes them go home and bring him back, against Jacob's best judgement. They start on a journey back to Joseph (Genesis 43), this time with Benjamin. Joseph visits with them, returning their silver in their packs, filling their packs with extra portions.

This time he schemes to keep Benjamin with him, so he plants his cup and has them brought back (Genesis 44), but he cannot keep up the story. He finally shares with his brothers who he is (Genesis 45). Joseph reveals himself to his brothers, wisely giving all credit to God.

4. If this was your story, what would you have done to your family? Would you have behaved as Joseph did? Why or why not?

_____

_____

_____

_____

_____

Genesis 45:4—24, Joseph shares with them that 'your selling me was of God. If I had not been, who would have provided for you?' He went on to share with them that I want my father close to me because this famine will last five more years and I don't want my family to die, yet they will benefit from my blessed life.

Pharaoh co-signed on the invitation and sent extra help to bring them back.

Joseph wisely gave all credit to God. His last piece of wisdom and advice was, "Don't quarrel on the way!" Again, wisdom tells Joseph that they will fight and blame each other. He told them that he had already forgiven them, permitting them to forgive themselves.

5. You have a family story. What is it? Does it prevent you from communications, extending your hand, loving them, or even weeping when you see them? What can you do to fix that?

_____
_____
_____
_____
_____

6. Have you forgiven them? Yourself? When will you do that?

_____
_____
_____
_____
_____

The sons had to come clean, confessing to their father what they did years ago (Genesis 45). The sons learned many lessons.

7. What did you learn? How will you use what you have learned? With whom will you share? With whom will you reconnect with because of these lessons?

___

Joseph is not the only wise one. Jacob hears from God (Genesis 46) who promises Jacob's trip to Egypt is best, and he will return to his home upon his death and Joseph will be there to close his eyes.
The sons also learned that their stunt did not solve their jealousy—Jacob still loved him intensely and intentionally. I would suggest that it was because of his heart and zeal, his intentions, and his investment, his love and forgiveness.

8. What did you learn about your new levels of wisdom after situations have come your way? What do you need to release in order to reach the next level of wisdom and to continue to find the Lord's favor?

___

Because of who Joseph was, the King extended his own resources toward this reunion. They were overwhelmed and completely humbled, even though the very dream that drove them to sin came true (Genesis 42:6). They had bowed before who they thought was a stranger, and had no problem with it. When they heard that they would bow before Joseph, they were indignant. But they did—they bowed before their brother, thought to be a stranger—who was there to provide for all of their needs.

Wise is Joseph, even at a young age to do the will of God, with the spirit of God, under the anointing of God, because of God's love. Joseph was a gracious ruler to even those he did not know. He never refused people for food. He bought their oxen, their land, and extended credit in order to feed them.

9. What have you learned from the character of Joseph? What will you do based on what you have read and learned in order to possess the character of Joseph?

_____

_____

_____

_____

10. The brothers still are at a misunderstanding. They believe that they are only blessed because of their father. They believe that now that dad is dead, that Joseph will change who he is by what he has done. Is that how families work? Is that how your family works? How should it work? What can you do to fix it?

_____
_____
_____
_____

Again, wise Joseph wept at their words. I question did Jacob really have to tell them to ask for forgiveness in verse 17. Jacob was also wise and knew the heart of his son. Did the sons create those words using their father's name as influence? I wonder when the brothers are going to grow up! The actions of Joseph could have been different. Most of us would not act like Joseph and further, Joseph had plenty of opportunity for revenge and it never crossed his heart nor mind!

11. Your thoughts: what would you do in your family to reconcile discord? Past, current, or future.

_____
_____
_____
_____
_____

The brothers do not understand Joseph, his love, nor his calling. Joseph just wants to love them and be loved by them.

What he states next changes the world: "You intended to harm me, but God intended it for good to accomplish what it now being done, the saving of many lives." Genesis 50:20.

That is one of the most profound statements ever made. And one of the wisest. Joseph just let them know that this is all about God. He demonstrates love, forgiveness, honor, and LOVE.

He lets them know that I did not do what I did just because of dad either. I will still provide for you.

God provided for some Israelites in a place that had previously harmed Israelites. It was not an act. It was a genuine love for his family, God and his position that he did all that he did. He did it because wisdom told him that he was working for a God that loves him and he has gained and had not ever lost anything in the process.

12. What did God show and teach you through Joseph? How will you change your heart, love and behavior as a result?

_____

_____

_____

_____

_____

13. How much wiser are you now? What will you do with that wisdom? Who will benefit and grow as a result of your wisdom?

_____
_____
_____
_____
_____

14. What is God calling you to do with what you are gifted with and now know?

_____
_____
_____
_____
_____

Bible Study for Women

Appendix

Your Testimony	204
The Names of God	206
Prayer Directions	208
Prayer Request List/Journal	209
Books and resources	213

Your Testimony

Your testimony is your experience with God and the results of that experience. This includes your first encounter with Christ to your current life.

Consider the answers to the following questions to develop your testimony:
1. When did you first meet Christ?
2. How do you share how you met Christ with others?
3. What have your encounters with God been like?
4. What is your relationship with God like?
5. What danger has He kept you from?
6. What have you done that would have sabotaged God's work if He had not stopped you?
7. What has happened that you realized that only God was in charge to make this happen?

_____

_____

_____

_____

_____

_____

_____

_____

_____

_____

_____

_____

_____

A Woman Like Me

The Names of God

(1) Elohim: The plural form of *EL*, meaning "strong one." It is used of false gods, but when used of the true God, it is a plural of majesty and intimates the trinity. It is especially used of God's sovereignty, creative work, mighty work for Israel and in relation to His sovereignty (Isa. 54:5; Jer. 32:27; Gen. 1:1; Isa. 45:18; Deut. 5:23; 8:15; Ps. 68:7).

Compounds of *El*:

- *El Shaddai:* "God Almighty." The derivation is uncertain. Some think it stresses God's loving supply and comfort; others His power as the Almighty one standing on a mountain and who corrects and chastens (Gen. 17:1; 28:3; 35:11; Ex. 6:1; Ps. 91:1, 2).
- *El Elyon:* "The Most High God." Stresses God's strength, sovereignty, and supremacy (Gen. 14:19; Ps. 9:2; Dan. 7:18, 22, 25).
- *El Olam:* "The Everlasting God." Emphasizes God's unchangeableness and is connected with His inexhaustibleness (Gen. 16:13).

(2) Yahweh (YHWH): Comes from a verb which means "to exist, be." This, plus its usage, shows that this name stresses God as the independent and self-existent God of revelation and redemption (Gen. 4:3; Ex. 6:3 (cf. 3:14); 3:12).

Compounds of *Yahweh:* Strictly speaking, these compounds are designations or titles which reveal additional facts about God's character.

- *Yahweh Jireh (Yireh):* "The Lord will provide." Stresses God's provision for His people (Gen. 22:14).
- *Yahweh Nissi:* "The Lord is my Banner." Stresses that God is our rallying point and our means of victory; the one who fights for His people (Ex. 17:15).
- *Yahweh Shalom:* "The Lord is Peace." Points to the Lord as the means of our peace and rest (Jud. 6:24).
- *Yahweh Sabbaoth:* "The Lord of Hosts." A military figure portraying the Lord as the commander of the armies of heaven (1 Sam. 1:3; 17:45).
- *Yahweh Maccaddeshcem*: "The Lord your Sanctifier." Portrays the Lord as our means of sanctification or as the one who sets believers apart for His purposes (Ex. 31:13).

- *Yahweh **Ro'i***: "The Lord my Shepherd." Portrays the Lord as the Shepherd who cares for His people as a shepherd cares for the sheep of his pasture (Ps. 23:1).
- *Yahweh **Tsidkenu***: "The Lord our Righteousness." Portrays the Lord as the means of our righteousness (Jer. 23:6).
- *Yahweh **Shammah***: "The Lord is there." Portrays the Lord's personal presence in the millennial kingdom (Ezek. 48:35).
- *Yahweh **Elohim Israel***: "The Lord, the God of Israel." Identifies Yahweh as the God of Israel in contrast to the false gods of the nations (Jud. 5:3.; Isa. 17:6).

(3) **Adonai:** Like *Elohim*, this too is a plural of majesty. The singular form means "master, owner." Stresses man's relationship to God as his master, authority, and provider (Gen. 18:2; 40:1; 1 Sam. 1:15; Ex. 21:1-6; Josh. 5:14).

(4) ***Theos***: Greek word translated "God." Primary name for God used in the New Testament. Its use teaches: (1) *He is the only true God* (Matt. 23:9; Rom. 3:30); (2) *He is unique* (1 Tim. 1:17; John 17:3; Rev. 15:4; 16:7); (3) *He is transcendent* (Acts 17:24; Heb. 3:4; Rev. 10:6); (4) *He is the Savior* (John 3:16; 1 Tim. 1:1; 2:3; 4:10). This name is used of Christ as God in John 1:1, 18; 20:28; 1 John 5:20; Tit. 2:13; Rom. 9:5; Heb. 1:8; 2 Pet. 1:1.

(5) ***Kurios***: Greek word translated "Lord." Stresses authority and supremacy. While it can mean sir (John 4:11), owner (Luke 19:33), master (Col. 3:22), or even refer to idols (1 Cor. 8:5) or husbands (1 Pet. 3:6), it is used mostly as the equivalent of *Yahweh* of the Old Testament. It too is used of Jesus Christ meaning (1) Rabbi or Sir (Matt. 8:6); (2) God or Deity (John 20:28; Acts 2:36; Rom. 10:9; Phil. 2:11).

(6) ***Despotes***: Greek word translated "Master." Carries the idea of ownership while *kurios* stressed supreme authority (Luke 2:29; Acts 4:24; Rev. 6:10; 2 Pet. 2:1; Jude 4).

(7) ***Father***: A distinctive New Testament revelation is that through faith in Christ, God becomes our personal Father. Father is used of God in the Old Testament only 15 times while it is used of God 245 times in the New Testament. As a name of God, it stresses God's loving care, provision, discipline, and the way we are to address God in prayer (Matt. 7:11; Jam. 1:17; Heb. 12:5-11; John 15:16; 16:23; Eph. 2:18; 3:15; 1 Thess. 3:11).

Source: http://www.agapebiblestudy.com/documents/the%20many%20names%20of%20god.htm

Bible Study for Women

Prayer
A Short How To Guide

The prayers which are most effective follow the following "rules:"

- It is a conversation with God.
- Be Honest with God.
- This is a relationship.
- God is to be praised, worshiped and glorified.
- God likes His word prayed back to Him.
- This is not a list of stuff you want.
- Think of more than yourself when you pray.
- Be authentic with God and yourself.
- Be prepared for people to ask you about your prayer life and faith.
- Do not worry about big words or long sentences.
- Please know that God is not taking revenge on others for you, and vice versa.
- Please prayer in the name of Jesus.
- There is no correct way to pray.

Scriptures on Prayer

Matthew 6:9-14

1 Thessalonians 5:17

Matthew 26:

John 17

Prayer Requests
Prayer Journal

1. What are you asking God for?
2. What are you hoping God will do?
3. What are you expecting from God?
4. What has God already done to exceed your expectations?
5. What has God done to get your attention?
6. What has He shown about Himself and you?

Bible Study for Women

A Woman Like Me

Resources

www.onediagage.com

Onediagagespeaks.com

Bible Study for Women

Acknowledgements

God, thank You for Your plans for me. Thank You for *A Woman Like Me: A Bible Study for Women,* and choosing me to complete Your project. I just want to please You, God. Thank You for continuing to anoint me and to invest in me and my gifts, which keep surprising me. Thank You for loving and forgiving me.

Hillary and Nehemiah, thank you for supporting me and my endeavors. Thank you for loving me, especially when I do nothing without a pen and a clipboard, thank you for enduring my late nights, your ideas, the sounding board, the love and the support. Thank you for celebrating our legacy.

To my prayer partners and to my accountability partners, thank you for the long talks and the powerful prayers and the encouragement.

To the readers who this will reach and empower and touch and affect, may these words empower you and help you reach some resolve. May you be inspired to achieve your goals and dreams. May you enhance your relationship with God so that your other relationships will also improve. May you enhance your self-esteem through prayer and study. May you have courage and peace. Share love the best you can until you can share love without reservation.

Bible Study for Women

About the Woman

As a woman who has been broken, hurt, rejected and unloved and who at some point done the breaking, hurting, rejecting, and unloving, we need to work to heal and that healing requires work. Work to heal. It is worth it to become whole. The author believes that this study will help you to grow and create the opportunity for you to grow closer to God and recover from your hurt.

Do not hesitate to ask, to engage at a high level of participation, anticipating God's best for you!

@onediagage (twitter) ♦ onediagage@onediagage.com ♦ facebook.com/onediagageministries
youtube.com/onediagage ♦ blogtalkradio.com/onediagage ♦ ongage (instagram)
www.onediagage.com ♦ www.onediagagebooks.com

Bible Study for Women

Preacher ♦ Advocate ♦ Teacher ♦ Facilitator
Conference Speaker ♦ Panelist ♦ Workshop Leader

To invite Rev. Gage to speak at your church, women's ministry,
Or other ministry.
Please contact us at: www.onedigage.com
@onediangage (twitter) ♦ onediagage@onediagage.com ♦ facebook.com/onediagageministries
youtube.com/onediagage ♦ blogtalkradio.com/onediagage ♦ ongage (Instagram)

Bible Study for Women

Publishing

Do you have a book you want to write, but do not know what to do?
Do you have a book you need to publish but do not know how to start?
Would publishing move your career forward?

Let us help

onediagage@purpleink.net ♦ www.purpleink.net

713.705.5530 ♦ 281.740.5143